Cambridge Elements

Elements in the Gothic
edited by
Dale Townshend
Manchester Metropolitan University
Angela Wright
University of Sheffield

GOTHIC VOICES

The Vococentric Soundworld of Gothic Writing

Matt Foley
Manchester Metropolitan University

CAMBRIDGE
UNIVERSITY PRESS

Shaftesbury Road, Cambridge CB2 8EA, United Kingdom

One Liberty Plaza, 20th Floor, New York, NY 10006, USA

477 Williamstown Road, Port Melbourne, VIC 3207, Australia

314–321, 3rd Floor, Plot 3, Splendor Forum, Jasola District Centre,
New Delhi – 110025, India

103 Penang Road, #05–06/07, Visioncrest Commercial, Singapore 238467

Cambridge University Press is part of Cambridge University Press & Assessment,
a department of the University of Cambridge.

We share the University's mission to contribute to society through the pursuit of
education, learning and research at the highest international levels of excellence.

www.cambridge.org
Information on this title: www.cambridge.org/9781009162562

DOI: 10.1017/9781009162579

First published 2023

A catalogue record for this publication is available from the British Library.

ISBN 978-1-009-16256-2 Paperback
ISSN 2634-8721 (online)
ISSN 2634-8713 (print)

Additional resources for this publication at www.cambridge.org/foley

Gothic Voices

The Vococentric Soundworld of Gothic Writing

Elements in the Gothic

DOI: 10.1017/9781009162579
First published online: January 2023

Matt Foley
Manchester Metropolitan University

Author for correspondence: Matt Foley, Matthew.Foley@mmu.ac.uk

Abstract: This Element provides new ways of reading the soundscape of the Gothic text. Drawing inspiration from the field of 'sonic Gothic' studies, which has been spearheaded by the writings of Isabella van Elferen, as well as from Mladen Dolar's articulation of the psychoanalytic 'object' voice, this study introduces the critical category of 'vococentric Gothic' into Gothic scholarship. In so doing, it reads important moments in Gothic fiction when the voice takes precedence as an uncanny, monstrous or seductive object. Historically informed, the range of readings proffered demonstrate the persistence of these vocal motifs across time (from the Gothic romance to contemporary Gothic) and across intermedia forms (from literature to film to podcasts). *Gothic Voices*, then, provides the first dedicated account of voices of terror and horror as they develop in the Gothic mode from the Romantic period until today.

Keywords: Gothic, voices, sonic Gothic, ventriloquism, vococentric

ISBNs: 9781009162562 (PB), 9781009162579 (OC)
ISSNs: 2634-8721 (online), 2634-8713 (print)

Contents

1 Impossible Voices

Since the age of the Gothic romance, which found its genesis in the mid-eighteenth century, disembodied, monstrous or uncanny voices have populated the soundworlds of literatures of terror and horror to this day. Such voices, in modern and contemporary times, have proliferated, too, in trans-media forms, including in radio, television, film and podcasting. In this Element, I suggest that several distinctive categories of representation of voice echo across Gothic texts. In so doing, I argue for an aesthetics of the voice and for the critical value of exploring and pursuing a new category – perhaps even subgenre – in Gothic studies that I term 'vococentric Gothic'. Essentially, vococentric Gothic is an auditory experience; if we listen attentively to Gothic texts, even literature, we realise that the voice can often take precedence over visual Gothic motifs. The importance of the Gothic soundworld to creating its signature atmospheres of suspense, terror or horror is understood by critics and audiences of the mode alike: creaking floorboards, howling winds and thunder rolling are just some of the acoustic motifs that alert us to a Gothic atmosphere. Vococentric Gothic, as I understand it, refers to the moments in Gothic fictions when the voice produces sublimity, terror, horror, awe, mystery, seduction and more.

To date, a number of prominent Gothic texts have received a good deal of scholarly attention in terms of their varied (and often haunting) representations of orality, including Charles Brockden Brown's *Wieland; or, The Transformation: An American Tale* (1798), the short stories of Edgar Allan Poe, George Du Maurier's *Trilby* (1894), Gaston Leroux's *The Phantom of the Opera* (1910) and Vernon Lee's 'A Wicked Voice' (1890).[1] A standout example of a nineteenth-century vococentric Gothic short story, Lee's rich narrative alerts us to the voice's role in art; its relationship to music; its function as muse and artistic inspiration; as well as the thematic, aesthetic and gendered ramifications of a castrato's 'queer' voice that haunts the narrator Magnus. The voice is a stain: an unwanted corruption of music and art that is nevertheless impossible to resist. Patricia Pulham's reading of 'A Wicked Voice' demonstrates the ways in which Lee's writing, with its persistent concerns of voice, music and the word, connects to psychoanalytic understandings of feminine

---

[1] I turn to such studies of Brockden Brown and Poe in the sections that follow. For a reading of the 'object voice' in *The Phantom of the Opera*, see Slavoj Žižek, *Enjoy Your Symptom!* 2nd ed. (London: Routledge, 2001), p. 114. For a fascinating account of the titular Trilby as a 'singing machine', see Fiona Coll, '"Just a Singing-Machine": The Making of an Automaton in George du Maurier's *Trilby*', *University of Toronto Quarterly* 79:2 (Spring 2010): 742–63. The title of Mladen Dolar's influential study *A Voice and Nothing More* (Cambridge, MA: MIT Press, 2006) is a quotation from Du Maurier's novel.

writing in which 'perhaps the voice's most threatening quality is its androgyny, for it is this hybridity which links its power to the threatening female voices of the past'.[2] 'A Wicked Voice', then, is a tale of excess and decadence in which the voice threatens established orders in a multitude of ways. The story's exuberant and multifaceted representation of the voice as persecutory, as an object of beauty and as an object of obsession speaks to a fundamental power of voice to metamorphosise and to engage our fears and desire in myriad guises. If narrative voice shapes the world we encounter, audible voices may penetrate this world's integrity, signifying change and, often in the Gothic and horror, creating disjuncture and conflict. To think of the voice in its fullest sense is to give in to this simultaneity of representation. The voice can be 'infernal' in one instant and in the next it may metamorphose into a melodic object of beauty: 'breaking itself in a shower of little scales and cadences and trills'.[3] From the nineteenth-century Gothic to modern and contemporary horrors, hybridity is one of the markers of the vococentric Gothic aesthetic across media.

1.1 Gothic Voices

Vococentric Gothic may be a new conceptual category for Gothic studies to attend to, but the practice of reading the voice's role in Gothic texts is already well underway. Jimmy Packham's *Gothic Utterance: Voice, Speech and Death in the American Gothic* (2021) provides the most extensive study in this area to date. In the only monograph published on the subject so far, Packham considers Gothic voices as they appear in late eighteenth- and nineteenth-century American Gothic. His argument reads a series of uncanny and disorderly voices that, in their alterity and in their various demands to be listened to, provoke a reshaping of boundaries between self and other, national identity and the human and technology in the fictions of an emerging American nation. By focusing on the 'reception' of Gothic voices in American culture, Packham argues persuasively for the 'absolute centrality of the voice and its utterances to the American Gothic tradition' as well as to the 'the literary project of America during its first century'.[4] Packham's carefully historicised and sustained reading of Gothicised orality in the fiction of Charles Brockden Brown, Edgar Allan Poe, Louisa May Alcott, Mary E Wilkins Freeman, Herman Melville and others opens up the possibility for a new field of Gothic studies to emerge. Packham

---

[2] Patricia Pulham, 'The Castrato and the Cry in Vernon Lee's Wicked Voices', *Victorian Literature and Culture* 30:2 (2002): 421–37 (p. 431).

[3] Vernon Lee, *Hauntings and Other Fantastic Tales*, eds. Catherine Maxwell and Patricia Pulham (Peterborough: Broadview Press, 2006), p. 166.

[4] Jimmy Packham, *Gothic Utterance: Voice, Speech and Death in the American Gothic* (Cardiff: University of Wales Press, 2021), p. 3.

reads Gothic voices as agents of transformation whereby voices of the dead or marginalised populaces can challenge and unpick 'easy or superficial distinctions between selves and their Others' in a series of representations that are 'invested in the promise ... to reinvent and reimagine prevailing relations, hierarchies, modes of being and so on'.[5] Packham's study, then, already implies that listening to the soundworld of the Gothic novel reveals it to be a vococentric mode.

One of the central ambitions of this Element is to demonstrate that vococentric Gothic operates beyond those Gothic texts that most obviously treat the voice as a mastertrope and as a sustained narrative concern. Vococentric Gothic, I suggest, encapsulates shorter narrative episodes, too, where the voice momentarily takes precedence, particularly when it is represented as disembodied, hybrid or ventriloquised. This rule holds for even the most excessive and visually grotesque of Gothic horrors, such as those moments of excess in William Peter Blatty's *The Exorcist* (1971), during which Regan MacNeil's voice becomes the monstrous auditory: a hybrid of human, demon and animal noises.[6] As we witness in William Friedkin's (1973) adaptation of Peter Blatty's novel, the demon Pazuzu's assault upon Regan's body is multitudinous, her weeping sores, varicose veins and sickly pallor all suggesting the decay and destruction of her flesh into something monstrous.[7] But her possession presents, too, an extreme and excessive version of a ventriloquial and demonic voice speaking through its young host. In Gothic and horror films, such monstrous (and hybrid) voices do not always sound from as clear a source; the voice can be produced offstage as it emanates from a mysterious 'other' place, which lies beyond the sight afforded to the viewer. This is the dynamic foregrounded often in theory-driven readings of the voice, particularly in Mladen Dolar and Slavoj Žižek's readings of Norma Bates's acousmatic voice presentation in Alfred Hitchcock's *Psycho* (1960). In pursuing their psychoanalytically informed accounts, Žižek and Dolar draw from the work of the aesthetic theories of Michel Chion, who,[8] in formulating his concepts of the acousmètre and acousmatic voice in film, introduces the idea of 'vococentric' cinema as 'the privilege accorded to the voice over all other sonic elements' in audiovisual media. In his introduction to *The Voice in Cinema* (1999), Chion further argues that 'Speech, shouts, sighs or whispers, the voice hierarchises everything around it.'[9]

---

[5] Packham, *Gothic Utterance*, p. 16.

[6] William Peter Blatty, *The Exorcist* (London: Corgi, 2007), pp. 125–6.

[7] *The Exorcist*, dir. William Friedkin (United States: Hoya Productions, 1973).

[8] See, for instance, Dolar, *A Voice and Nothing More*, pp. 60–2.

[9] Michel Chion, *The Voice in Cinema*, trans. Claudia Gorbman (New York: Columbia University Press, 1999), p. 6.

Articulation therefore creates an order, so to speak, by its very production by distinguishing itself from ambient sound as the bearer of some message or communication. Chion refers to film narration. Gothic vococentrism locates the voice as a privileged object, too – one that often penetrates and sounds through a suspenseful Gothic atmosphere.

In current scholarship, there is little consideration of the intertextual dimensions to Gothic voices and to the larger soundworld their textual connections create; instead, their representations are traced more readily to authorial or technological contexts and concerns. Recent work in the field of sonic Gothic, which reads primarily the literary aesthetic, has explored the acoustics of particular Gothic romances,[10] the short stories of Poe and the soundscape of the Victorian Gothic.[11] However elucidating their findings may be, this series of critical readings is often not explicitly connected to the development of the Gothic mode itself, and none provide an overarching account of vococentric Gothic from the Romantic period to the present. Much of the work to date on Victorian Gothic soundscapes, for instance, characterises the terror fiction of the period as responding to a supposedly disconcerting series of changes in listening cultures and technologies, from the invention of the telegraph to the telephone and the phonograph. Yet, as John Picker argues with regard to the emergence of the phonograph in the late nineteenth century, the 'mechanical reproduction of voice ... offered forms of control and interaction that late Victorians initially found not impersonal and fearful as moderns often did, but, in a period of diminishing mastery over empire and the self, individualized, reassuring and even desirable'.[12] Even as they acknowledge the nuances of historical context, as Picker's argument does with great care, critical accounts of the disembodied, spectral or technologised voices of the period overlook that these Victorian oralities reiterate an aestheticisation of the voice foundational to the first Gothic romances published in the eighteenth century. When asked, in 1888, to record a piece on Thomas Edison's 'perfected' phonograph for George

---

[10] See Peter Weisse, 'The Object Voice in Romantic Irish Novels', in Jorge Sacido-Romero and Sylvia Mieszkowski (eds.), *Sound Effects: The Object Voice in Fiction* (Leiden: Brill Rodopi, 2015), pp. 47–71; Joan Passey, 'The Aesthetics of the Auditory: Sound and Silence in the Novels of Ann Radcliffe', *Horror Studies* 7:2 (2016): 189–204; Angela M. Archambault, 'The Function of Sound in the Gothic Novels of Ann Radcliffe, Matthew Lewis and Charles Maturin', *Études Épistémè* 29 (June 2016), http://journals.openedition.org/episteme/965 [last accessed 11 April 2021].

[11] See Fred Botting, 'Poe, Voice, and the Origin of Horror Fiction', in Jorge Sacido-Romero and Sylvia Mieszkowski (eds.), *Sound Effects: The Object Voice in Fiction* (Leiden: Brill Rodopi, 2015), pp. 73–100; Frances Clarke, 'Gothic Vibrations and Edgar Allan Poe', *Horror Studies* 7:2 (2016): 205–17. See Kristie A. Schlauraff, 'Victorian Gothic Soundscapes', *Literature Compass* 15:4 (2018), https://onlinelibrary.wiley.com/doi/full/10.1111/lic3.12445 [last accessed 17 April 2021].

[12] John Picker, *Victorian Soundscapes* (Oxford: Oxford University Press, 2003), p. 113.

Edward Gouraud's collection of recordings, the great Shakespearean actor Henry Irving, who was accompanied by his manager Bram Stoker at the time and would go on to be an inspiration for Count Dracula, chose to recite part of Matthew Gregory Lewis's Gothic monodrama *The Captive* (1803). Picker notes that '[i]n his choice of this scene for recitation, Irving intuitively gestured to the as yet unexplored way the phonograph would become a prison-house for spoken language'.[13] Perhaps Irving's 'intuition' sensed the shared fascination that visitors to Gouraud's library would have for technologised Gothic voices. The relevance of the received, and not just the modern Victorian, Gothic to these nineteenth-century experiences of technology should not be overlooked. Furthermore, nineteenth-century audiences would have been familiar, too, with other forms of uncanny voices through their encounters with the practice and performance of ventriloquism; these are uncanny voices that the human body could produce without technological enhancement.

1.2 Ventriloquism

The few critical examinations published so far that explore the influence of the *act* of ventriloquism upon anglophone nineteenth-century Gothic literature all resist this temptation to frame the voice as primarily phonographic, telephonic or technologised. Produced by skilled and natural means, distant voice ventriloquism was an important and popular strand to late eighteenth- and nineteenth-century theatre and literature. The ventriloquist would 'throw' their voice offstage, or into props, creating the illusion of a conversation. This technique was clearly of interest to writers of the supernatural. Distant voice ventriloquism was discussed by Sir Walter Scott in his *Letters on Demonology and Witchcraft* (1830); it was also alluded to, and appropriated by, Poe in his short fiction, explicitly so in his late detective story 'Thou Art the Man' (1844), which I read at more length in Section 3. Scott, too, was acquainted with the world-famous ventriloquist Alexandre Vattemare, who visited him at Abbotsford and to whom he wrote a dedicatory epigram, while Poe attended the ventriloquist shows of Signor Blitz in Philadelphia and would most likely have read David Brewster's response to Scott's letters that explores the 'natural magic' of ventriloquism in even more detail.[14] Ventriloquism forms part of a nineteenth-century aural culture of entertainment – a wider culture that writers such as Charles Dickens, who toured relentlessly, actively participated in through performances and readings of their writing. Even if we cannot be certain that

---

[13] Picker, *Victorian Soundscapes*, p. 119.

[14] Susan Sweeney, 'Echoes of Ventriloquism in Poe's Tales', *Poe Studies: History, Theory, Interpretation* 54:1 (2021): 127–55 (p. 130).

Dickens attended ventriloquist shows, he would almost certainly have been aware of them and the popular literature that they spawned, such as Henry Cockton's *The Life and Adventures of Valentine Vox, the Ventriloquist* (1839).

The practice of ventriloquism is particularly open for Gothicisation as it decouples any socially pervasive understanding that one's voice is a marker of coherent subjectivity; it also denaturalises the relationship between the voice and the space from which it emanates. This Gothicisation of voice throwing is evident in Brewster's repost to Scott, in which he provides an account of mischievous trickery undertaken in a Parisian convent by the ventriloquist Saint-Gille. Drawing his account from Jean-Baptiste de la Chapelle's late eighteenth-century history of the art form, *Le ventriloque, ou l'engastrimythe* (1772), Brewster writes that Saint-Gille

> had occasion to shelter himself from a storm in a neighbouring convent, where the monks were in deep mourning for a much-esteemed member of their community who had been recently buried. While lamenting over the tomb of their deceased brother the slight honours which had been paid to his memory, a voice was suddenly heard to issue from the roof of the choir bewailing the condition of the deceased in purgatory, and reproving the brotherhood for their want of zeal ... the whole convent fell upon their faces, and vowed to make a reparation of their error. They accordingly chanted in full choir a *De Profundis*, during the intervals of which the spirit of the departed monk expressed his satisfaction at their pious exercises.[15]

This account of vocal deception certainly wears the clothes of an eighteenth-century Gothic narrative: a nunnery, death, monastic dedication and the solemn chanting of *De Profundis* are all present, to name but a few of the motifs that would become associated with the British Gothic romance that are on display in Brewster's telling. Yet, Saint-Gille's voice throwing, which mocks rather than scares, can be considered a truly Gothic act in only one way: he mimics the dead. In establishing its Gothic connotations, the setting of this voice-throwing vignette is just as important, perhaps more so than Saint-Gille's ventriloquial act. What this passage draws stark attention to, however, is that disembodied and acousmatic voices *demand* action from their listeners, and that they carry something suggestive of a supernatural power. These Gothic voices disorientate as they disrupt space, emanating often from obscured sources, which are often assumed to be associated with divine power.

Mirroring the tale of Saint-Gille, the Gothic's recurring depictions of disembodied voices are tied often to its architecture of place. Distant voices call from occluded or forbidden spaces: attics, basements, prisons, subterranean vaults

---

[15] David Brewster, *Letters on Natural Magic: Addressed to Sir Walter Scott* (London: John Murray, 1834), p. 172.

and so on. As Steven Connor has suggested, the voice 'inhabits and occupies space; and it also actively procures space for itself', its demands and calls seeking to locate a listener and to be heard. Elaborating, Connor advocates for new conceptualisations of what he terms 'vocalic space' – a way of framing these relationships – where 'the voice is held both to operate in, and itself to articulate, different conceptions of space, as well as to enact the different relations between the body, community, time, and divinity'.[16] The Gothic not only takes advantage of the voice's relationship to space – the way in which it can extend the power of its speaker – but we might also say that it creates vocalic atmospheres, through its recurring representations of acoustic motifs of balladry, chanting and disembodied voices. The contradictions of reading voice as space are as important as they are disorientating; the effects of acts of ventriloquism rely upon a spatial deficit between the aural sense and sight. As Connor argues, ventriloquism has 'an active and a passive form, depending upon whether it is thought of as the power to speak through others or as the experience of being spoken through by others'.[17] In vococentric Gothic, we find that ventriloquism takes often a passive form in figures of possession; only more rarely do characters engage in sustained trickery via aural deception, such as in the figure of the biloquist Carwin in *Wieland*. While Connor's study makes clear that the history of ventriloquism is complex and multifaceted, very little reference is made to its influence upon Gothic fiction. Clearly, there are Gothic acts of ventriloquism that are represented in literature from its earliest novels, but it is the second of Connor's categories that has wider significance for the Gothic. Being 'spoken through by others' is the essence of Gothic representations of possession, madness and the mediumship of ghosts.

1.3 Transformative Listening

In subsequent sections, my argument will often be concerned with reading vococentric Gothic as a literature of excess in its many representations of guttural or presymbolic voices, but an important function of the uncanny voice, particularly in ghost stories, is that it can be radical and transformative while still being articulate. Published first in *Blackwood's Magazine*, Margaret Oliphant's vococentric Gothic tale 'The Open Door' (1882) presents an opening up to spectrality – a speaking with the ghost – that is transformative to the living *and* the dead. In Oliphant's tale, speaking with the apparition challenges and recasts pervasive 'modern' belief systems borne out of the Scottish Enlightenment. The story demonstrates the

---

[16] Steven Connor, *Dumbstruck: A Cultural History of Ventriloquism* (Oxford: Oxford University Press, 2000), pp. 12–3.

[17] Connor, *Dumbstruck*, p. 14.

power of listening attentively to the Gothic voice. The tale's first-person narrator, Colonel Mortimer, is a disciple of middle-class, professional and Enlightened thought who patently believes in the primacy of rationalisation; nevertheless, he comes to learn from his son Roland that the ghostly can be attended to in a way that not merely challenges but expands his ontological belief system.[18] Roland's name is of heroic stature and he is consistently feminisied; this is a productive femininity that his father comes to adopt. As such, Enlightenment masculinity is dislocated from patriarchal belief systems and this transformation is achieved through attentive modes of listening. After travelling to the ruins where his son first heard a spectral voice, Mortimer discovers a 'spirit in pain – if it was a spirit' that is recognised as an oral and auditory phenomenon *first*: 'this voice out of the unseen – was a poor fellow-creature in misery, to be succoured and helped out of his trouble'.[19] It is the praxis of *listening* empirically and of trusting the auditory sense that leads the father to a realisation akin to Horatio's in William Shakespeare's *Hamlet* (1603): there are more things in heaven and earth, this story suggests, than are accounted for in Enlightenment philosophies. Luke Thurston describes the spectre's speech as a 'threshold voice' emanating from the ruined home, one that calls to a narrator who himself is located on an 'ideological threshold' that presents an opportunity to be transformed by alterity.[20]

As Scott Brewster observes, 'Oliphant's ghost stories suggest that intimacy is found through estrangement, and opening up to the Other need not involve fear'.[21] To be intimate with the ghost is a decisively ethical and transformative act that is auditory in nature. In surveying nineteenth-century Scottish Gothic, Brewster reads the spectral encounter of 'The Open Door' alongside the writings of James Hogg and Robert Louis Stevenson to examine the Scottish ghost story's mirroring of what Jacques Lacan terms 'extimacy' – that is, an intimate yet unnerving and *external* experience with the other that, given its association with Gothic doubling, elides any notion that the self can be clearly delineated from what it professes not to be.[22] It is only through *work* that one can truly learn from the spectral other. That work may mean conversing with and attending to an other who, when first encountered, terrifies or horrifies us. By the end of the tale, any scepticism towards the existence of the ghost is painted as narrow-minded, and itself delusionary. The belief that this

[18] Luke Thurston, 'Stories Not Like Any Others: Ghosts and the Ethics of Literature', in Scott Brewster and Luke Thurston (eds.), *The Routledge Handbook to the Ghost Story* (London: Routledge, 2017), pp. 467–75 (pp. 471–2).

[19] Margaret Oliphant, *The Open Door and Other Stories of the Seen and Unseen*, ed. Mike Ashley (London: The British Library, 2021), p. 119.

[20] Thurston, 'Stories Not Like Any Others', p. 473.

[21] Scott Brewster, 'Extimacies: Strange Attachments in James Hogg, Robert Louis Stevenson, and Margaret Oliphant', *Gothic Studies* 24:1 (2022): 57–69 (p. 64).

[22] Brewster, 'Extimacies', p. 58

haunting could be theatrical artifice, even the act of a ventriloquist, is judged negatively by the narrator when he observes it in Roland's doctor, Simson: 'The miserable voice, the spirit in pain, [Simson] could think of as the result of ventriloquism, or reverberation, or – anything you please: an elaborate prolonged hoax, executed somehow by the tramp that had found a lodging in the old tower.'[23] Oliphant's tale takes us to the very threshold of reasoned and reasonable listening in order to transgress these limits, offering up a more radical ontology – one that is close to what Jacques Derrida has referred to as a *hauntology* – that pays heed to what is absent, present and in-between in the physical and the spectral world. Such attentive listening out for and to the spectral voice is itself an ethical act.

In adopting a methodology of 'listening' to Gothic literature throughout this Element, I draw from certain understandings of listening as praxis, which have been articulated in the field of sound studies. In *The Audible Past* (2003), his history of sound recording and reproduction, Jonathan Sterne argues for a recalibration of the models of cause and effect that have traditionally shaped studies that explore the influence of sonic technologies upon culture. Importantly, Sterne does not privilege technology as the source from which may spring fresh understandings of sound and listening. Instead, he argues that 'new sound technologies had an impact on the nature of sound or hearing, but they were part of social and cultural currents'.[24] While Sterne's ideas may liberate us from privileging technological developments over broader cultural production, his overarching definition of sound reminds us of a limit to the compatibility of his field of study with literary acoustics: for Sterne, 'sound is a class of vibration that might be heard'.[25]

The phenomenological problem that lies at the heart of the application of sound studies to literary acoustics is that the former field's functional understanding of sound seems incompatible with the latter's status as representation. Yet, in a move that is useful for literary analysis, Sterne understands 'audible' to mean 'a person in whom "auditory images" are predominant over tactile and visual stimuli' and transposes this definition into a scholarly category that denotes 'hearing and listening as developed and specialised practices, rather than inherent capacities'.[26] The close linguistic association between Sterne's interest in 'auditory images' and Ferdinand de Saussure's influential account of the signifier as a sound image in his *Lectures on General Linguistics* (1916) is obvious. Perhaps more importantly, Sterne furnishes the critical practice of 'listening' with a series of connotations that may be read as epistemological starting points for scholarly engagement with literary soundscapes. Underpinning the practice of sound studies, 'listening' becomes 'a directed, learned activity: it is a definite cultural

---

[23] Oliphant, *The Open Door and Other Stories*, p. 120.

[24] Jonathan Sterne, *The Audible Past* (Durham: Duke University Press, 2003), p. 35.

[25] Sterne, *The Audible Past*, p. 11.   [26] Sterne, *The Audible Past*, p. 96.

practice. Listening requires hearing but is not simply reducible to hearing'.[27] The diachronic and intertextual nature of the Gothic's reiteration of a series of its signature soundscapes means that these soundworlds often resist being read via a cause-and-effect historical analysis. As such, representations of troubling voices in the Gothic are transhistorical in the sense that they recur across a series of intertextual relations that often defy periodicity and historical boundaries.

Patently, any act of reading creates an interpretative relationship between the mind and the signifier, between the mind's ear, as it were, and what the eye sees on the page. Studies of the acoustics of the literary text understandably approach the question of just how text produces sound heard by the mind's ear tentatively and with care. One such example is Angela Leighton's *Hearing Things: The Work of Sound in Literature* (2018), which focuses on the peculiarly sonic nature of poetry. As Leighton puts it, in an act of reading, 'the ear hovers somewhere between a literal and a metaphorical faculty in the work of reading, between a sense perception, alert to real noises, and a figure for hearing which might pay attention to sounds on the page that are self-evidently inaudible'.[28] Reading sharpens our perception, creating an alertness to representations of sound and to the acoustic aura produced by text. Gothic texts revel in heightening the senses and elicit in their readerships a desire to *know*; they promise reward, revelation and even horror. And the revelations we crave might be uttered – be that in a whisper, a confession or a pleading scream.

In her introduction to *Hearing Things*, Angela Leighton draws together work on the acoustics of poetry to emphasise that attentive listening takes us towards the very limits of the audible. As in Oliphant's 'The Open Door', such limits can be porous, inviting transgression and going beyond them can open new vistas of experience. Recalling, then, the heightening of senses experienced during moments of terror and suspense in the Gothic, for instance in a heroine's tentative approach to a secret or occluded chamber, attentive listening is a straining of the senses or analytical faculties that compels us to confront the limits of what can and cannot be heard. As Leighton puts it:

> Beyond what is technically called "the threshold of audibility" lies the huge, unheard "sound shadow" of noises outside our range: those too high or too low for human detection, or just too far away. Thresholds are a limit as well as an opening. When thinking about the complexities of listening to and in literature, the notion of thresholds as places of passage and blockage, corridors and doors, might become a suggestive working metaphor for the kinds of attention demanded by the literary text.[29]

---

[27] Sterne, *The Audible Past*, p. 19.
[28] Angela Leighton, *Hearing Things: The Work of Sound in Literature* (Cambridge, MA: Harvard University Press, 2018), p. 2.
[29] Leighton, *Hearing Things*, p. 22.

Such a testing of boundaries is a highly Gothicised scenario; its emphasis upon heightened sensory perception amidst exploring 'corridors and doors' as thresholds resonates with an aesthetic of suspense. Indeed, Leighton makes direct reference to the Gothic and ghost stories throughout her study, noting, for instance, 'that sound lends itself to a vocabulary of the preternatural. While the sense of sight verifies without any need for interpretation, hearing, with its often surmised or memorized location of origins, slips easily into a more distant apprehension, memory, or sometimes even imagination of a sound'.[30] Leighton takes up the work of David Toop here, whose *Sinister Resonance* (2010) adopts a personalised, thoughtful and critical/creative approach to exploring the affects and effects of sound in literature and film. As Toop's title suggests, the connections that we feel between ourselves and the soundworld produced by Gothic texts are often as unnerving as they are appealing. Terror and horror fiction activate our desire even as they fill us with fear and apprehension.

1.4 The Gothic Soundworld

Following Walter Murch's emphasis on the pre-symbolic or 'preternatural' exposure to sound that we have in the womb, Toop explores Gothic and haunting soundworlds by beginning from a premise that resonates, too, with the conceptual framework proffered in Isabella van Elferen's *Gothic Music: The Sounds of the Uncanny* (2012). Van Elferen's study is foundational to the field of sonic Gothic studies, and its argument shares Toop's understanding that sound itself is spectral given its invisibility and intangibility. This ghostly quality is tied to space; a distant sound, particularly where its origin is occluded, is patently spectral. Toop's formulation of 'distant music' – a phrase drawn from James Joyce's description of Greta Conroy as she lingers on the Morkans' staircase in 'The Dead' (1914) – is replete with connotations that help us locate a meeting point between spectral haunting, sound and personal and cultural history: this is 'a reaching back into the lost places of the past, the slippages and mirages of memory, history reaching forward in the intangible form of sound to reconfigure the present and future'.[31] In Van Elferen's landmark study of the Gothic's transmedia soundworld, voices are a constant point of analysis, and often they are described in hauntological terms. Importantly, Van Elferen sees a connection between the uncanny and disembodied spoken voice and its more melodic counterpoint. 'Gothic spectres', she argues, 'are often audible before they become visible, and their ephemeral voices are all the more chilling when they sing'. Van Elferen goes on to characterise Cathy's auditory haunting in Emily Brontë's *Wuthering Heights* (1847), and her refrain of 'Let me in – let me

---

[30] Leighton, *Hearing Things*, p. 4.

[31] David Toop, *Sinister Resonance: The Mediumship of the Listener* (London: Bloomsbury, 2010), p. 9.

in!', as an 'emblem of ghostliness',[32] one that echoes through the pages, stages and screens of the countless Gothic adaptations of Brontë's novel. The airy, disembodied and melodic voices of the Gothic to which van Elferen refers are often eerie but rarely truly frightening; even atonal singing – or the atonal striking of a piano key or string in a film score – cannot be said to be horrific. Truly unruly voices in the Gothic are fully embodied, their monstrosity suggesting excess drive rather than unsatiated desire: an excess of the body that threatens to overpower the symbolic and social functions of the voice.

In this vein, no horror soundworld is complete without a scream (Sound 1), the purest representation of the voice stripped of its symbolic content, flooding through space as a powerful stream of noise: a last defence when all is lost, and the body must flee. Screaming voices in the Gothic represent a ferocious abjection of the rational self, but they also act as a beacon or a signal that extends the space and reach of corporeality in peril. In Section 4, I read the Gothic scream across the three connected intermedial soundworlds of Robert Bloch, Alfred Hitchcock and Bernard Herrmann's versions of *Psycho*. Tracing Janet Leigh's emblematic horror screams back to Bloch's novel, which Hitchcock adapted very soon after its publication in 1959, we find that there is a curious absence of noise in the original. In Bloch's text, Mary's (the original of Hitchcock's Marion) scream is cut off and the limits of the acoustic text are reached. Stripped of metaphor, the scream has no description, as if words alone cannot do justice to the sound. Norman's *possession* by Norma Bates – his hearing and articulation of his mother's voice – in Bloch's novel draws at least some of its ventriloquial force from the acoustic and vocal sensibilities of the fiction of Edgar Allan Poe, which I read in Section 3. By comparing Poe's monstrous voices to Dickens's ghost voices in this section, we see very clearly what is at stake when uncanny and monstrous voices sound in the nineteenth-century text. The two ventriloquial categories of 'active' and 'passive' voicing are, in psychoanalytic discourse, deeply connected through their shared representation of the voice as an object, one that we can see running throughout the soundworlds of the first Gothic novels that I read in the next section, and in horror podcasting that I turn to reading in the conclusion to this study.

Sound 1 'Scream.mp3'. Audio file available at www.cambridge.org/foley
Source: Grez1, *Free Sound*. Available online: https://freesound.org/people/Grez1/
sounds/485802

---

[32] Isabella van Elferen, *Gothic Music: The Sounds of the Uncanny* (Cardiff: University of Wales Press, 2012), pp. 4, 21.

The argument that follows in this Element, then, contributes to a conceptual framework that is currently in development in Gothic studies, through which we can read Gothic voices as they appear in transmedial, transhistorical and transnational contexts. Three motifs of vocality, I argue, are central to the Gothic and the effects (and affects) that it produces across media: that is, monstrous, uncanny and ventriloquised representations of the voice. What unites these acoustic motifs – within the framework of the narrative worlds in which they sound – is that they are all considered *impossible* voices. Each in its own way, the examples that I read in this Element confound the rational laws of the worlds in which they appear: the spectral voices of Ann Radcliffe's fiction; the noisy Bleeding Nun of Matthew Gregory Lewis's *The Monk* (1796); the infernal voice of Charles Robert Maturin's Faustian Melmoth in *Melmoth the Wanderer* (1820); the psychic hallucinations of Charles Brockden Brown's *Wieland*; the penetrating voice of Robert Bloch's Norma Bates and so on. To borrow a phrase from Mladen Dolar's psychoanalytic account of the voice and its alterity, these are fictions in which the effects of the voice exceed their probable causes.[33] The readings of vococentric Gothic that I offer across this Element are intended to be representative; they are windows into what can be revealed if we listen attentively to Gothic voices. They provide a glimpse into an intertextual Gothic soundworld that is multifaceted and connected across texts and across time. Helen Davies has made clear that 'in attempting to define ventrilo-quism' there emerges a 'tension between "transformation" and "repetition"'.[34] There is a comparable tension between modern and contemporary Gothic and the literary heritage that came before it. Literal figurations of ventriloquism or voice throwing arise in the Gothic alongside, and often as products of, an intertextual ventriloquism of Gothic tropes, sounds and atmospheres past. Soundscapes of Gothic texts, then, share a series of acoustic motifs across time that together form a larger, intertextual Gothic soundworld of repetition and transformation.

2 Thrilling Groans and Attentive Listening: Vococentric Gothic Romance

This section surveys, and critically locates, several of the most important forms of vococentric Gothic in the early Gothic romance (c.1765–1820) by examining the ways in which seductive, uncanny, tyrannical and inarticulate voices shape the genre's soundworld and narrative structures.[35] Paying attention to Romantic

---

[33] Dolar, *A Voice and Nothing More*, p. 70.

[34] Helen Davies, *Gender and Ventriloquism in Victorian and Neo-Victorian Fiction: Passionate Puppets* (Houndmills: Palgrave Macmillan, 2012), p. 6.

[35] For a classic critical account of the Gothic's seductive narrative structures see Beth Newman, 'Narratives of Seduction and the Seductions of Narrative: The Frame Structure of *Frankenstein*', *English Literary History* 53 (1986): 141–61.

aesthetics, my argument here draws from Ann Radcliffe's definitions of terror and obscurity, as put forth in her posthumously published 'On the Supernatural in Poetry' (1826), and recasts these for the Gothic soundworld by placing them alongside James Beattie's understandings of sanitised and unruly voices. In the Gothic, if an object is presented as 'obscure' to sight or to the aural sense, it tends to generate a sense of mystery, promoting a heightening of the senses as it does so: terror, intertwined with curiosity, ensues. An experience of terror or suspense opens-up the potential for sublime revelation. Radcliffe's contemporary, the Scottish philosopher James Beattie and his theories of sublimity are well known to Gothic scholars.[36] Beattie shares Edmund Burke's recognition that atmospheric sounds – such as thunder – can be a source of sublimity. Yet, his interest in aesthetics and mimicry takes him beyond the parameters of Burkean thought and his theories of the pleasures derived from voice, music and poetry offered important understandings of 'imitation' and 'natural voice' that can be juxtaposed with the more unruly oralities of vococentric Gothic. As Dale Townshend has noted, Romantic aesthetics may have been ostensibly 'characterised by a concerted privileging of the voice' in opposition to the visual registers of the Gothic romance,[37] but there is a persistent and important strand to Gothic aesthetics that is concerned with voice, too: not the purifying poetic voice of Romantic poetry, per se, but, instead, a series of disconcerting and uncanny oralities. Indeed, many of the concerns of vococentric Gothic as they still pertain today find their genesis in the writings of Ann Radcliffe, William Godwin, Charles Maturin, Charles Brockden Brown and other writers of the Gothic romance. This section, then, elaborates upon Beattie's understanding of noise as being antagonist towards the melodious, mimetic voice by considering how the 'inharmonious' Gothic voices in terror literature are transformed from noise into human utterance, while in Gothic horror of the Romantic period such representations of orality retain their alterity and, in so doing, foreground the transformative potential of seductive and infernal voices.

The often excessive visual dimensions of the Gothic novel have long been scrutinised by critics, whether that be to attack the Gothic as a low-cultural form of 'beggarly day-dreaming', as Samuel Taylor Coleridge did in *Biographia Literaria* (1817),[38] or to explore the mode's continuing predilection for displaying visual excesses, such as the sublime landscapes of Ann Radcliffe's fiction or

---

[36] An extract from Beattie's 'Illustrations on Sublimity' appears, for instance, in Rictor Norton (ed.), *Gothic Readings: The First Wave, 1764–1840* (London: Leicester University Press, 2000), pp. 283–5.

[37] Dale Townshend, 'Gothic Visions, Romantic Acoustics', *Romantic Circles*, December 2005, www.rc.umd.edu/praxis/gothic/townshend/townshend, para 1 [last accessed 20 April 2022].

[38] Cited in Townshend, 'Gothic Visions, Romantic Acoustics', para 5.

the porous, graphic corporealities of a writer such as Matthew Lewis.[39] The
Gothic, in its first incarnation in the late eighteenth century, was inspired by
a visionary dream: Horace Walpole's night-time imagining of 'a gigantic hand
in armour' placed on the 'uppermost staircase' of 'an ancient castle', which
prompted Walpole to work feverishly on *The Castle of Otranto* (1765).[3] After
Walpole, the Gothic romance of the late eighteenth century deployed promin-
ently and consistently the narrative device of the portentous dream of forebod-
ing as a method of prolepsis, one that locates the unconscious (at least as we
may term it now) as a place of profound if troubling truth and a locus in which
prohibited desires may find expression.[4] Lewis's *The Monk*, for instance, is
replete with a series of troubling dreams that, at least according to
D. L. Macdonald, are 'both psychologically plausible and premonitory ...
either natural or supernatural'.[40] In her introduction to the 1831 edition of
Frankenstein; or, The Modern Prometheus, Mary Shelley famously recounted
another inspirational, if morbid, 'waking' dream that inspired the writing of her
creature's birth. It is tempting to approach the Gothic, then, as a dream (or
nightmare) literature itself.

Inspired by its author's dream, the soundworld of the first self-proclaimed
Gothic novel, Horace Walpole's *The Castle of Otranto*, is dominated by the
voice – be that in the supernatural 'groaning' that echoes throughout Otranto
and signals injustice and false inheritance, or in the tyrannical voice of Manfred,
the false Prince, that regulates the desire of others and bears his perverse and
incestuous demands. The atmosphere of the supernatural that permeates the
novel includes a rather absurd and inarticulate voice. A 'deep and hollow groan'
startles Matilda and Theodore as they discuss transgressing the law of the tyrant,
Matilda's father, Manfred. The 'hollowness' of this voice is particularly telling:
it seems evacuated of any real terror or horror. Rather than being the result of
'pent-up vapours', as the absurd explanation provided by Walpole's narrator
suggests, it is clearly an indicator of the supernatural, a sourceless and other-
worldly groan detached from human corporeality.[41] In the early Gothic novel,
a moan may act as a demand or call for justice. Often, the disembodied moan
belongs to a *locus* that is beyond the field of the characters' – and the reader's –
vison. Aligning with her signature motif of the explained supernatural, the
ghostly voices that reverberate throughout Radcliffe's *A Sicilian Romance*

[39] For an overview of these concerns, see the introductory chapter to Fred Botting, *Gothic*, 2nd ed.
(London: Routledge, 2013).
[40] D. L. Macdonald "'A Dreadful Dreadful Dream": Transvaluation, Realization, and Literalization
of *Clarissa* in *The Monk*', *Gothic Studies*, 6:2 (2004): 157–71.
[41] Horace Walpole, *The Castle of Otranto*, ed. Nick Groom (Oxford: Oxford University Press,
2014), p.68.

(1790) are eventually revealed to be the cries of a wronged woman incarcerated in a prohibited wing of the Castle Mazzini. Louisa Bernini's spectral voice produces 'low and dismal' noise that, as Radcliffe describes it, is carried by 'intervals' of 'hollow sighings'; the profound revelation that sourcing this acousmatic voice has upon the narrative is signalled by the very depth of the voice and the response it produces from Ferdinand, the son of Bernini. Imprisoned in the vaults, he listens in 'deep amazement' to the 'deep distress' of his mother; the timbre and tone of the mother's cries are spatial insofar as they penetrate through the walls of her prison.[42] The voice's very movement positions it as a transformative vocalic object that penetrates space; if listened to carefully, it has the potential to reorganise, and indeed usurp, the prevailing power dynamics that support the tyranny of Ferdinand Mazzini. Indeed, this is what happens once the source of the acousmatic voice is found – and the mother's role is resurrected.

The distinction between the eventually sourced and localised voice in Radcliffe and seemingly sourceless voice in Walpole reflects and contributes to the texts' different attitudes to the supernatural. In typically Radcliffean fashion, at first the imprisoned mother's wails are thought to be the ghostly howls of a disquieted spirit, until the supernatural is explained away by the emergence of a hitherto hidden injustice perpetrated by a tyrannical figure, the Marquis of Mazzini himself. In Walpole's *Otranto*, the threat is more pervasive and existential, the fall of the tyrant Manfred fated by a higher power. An omniscient force rights the sins of the father and restores the familial heritage of Theodore, who is revealed to be the legitimate Prince of Otranto.[43] Thus, the literature of terror (Radcliffe) and the literature of horror (Walpole) may often evoke comparable soundscapes, but the function – if not the form – of these auditory elements differ in accordance with such texts' handling of the super-natural. Through Gothic groans, the a-symbolic side to the voice becomes pronounced; but such an example of pure vocal affect can still signify even where articulate words are impossible to discern. In Walpole, the groan is a sign that the 'time is out of joint', and that fate itself has been affronted by Manfred's usurpation of the throne. In Radcliffe, the mother's moans indicate, too, an injustice from the past that remains hidden in the present – and the effects of these Radcliffean injustices are intimate and mournful. In both Walpole and Radcliffe, acousmatic voices are described as 'hollow'; they carry a-symbolic

---

[42] Ann Radcliffe, *A Sicilian Romance*, ed. Alison Milbank (Oxford: Oxford University Press, 2008), pp. 96–7.

[43] For a fuller articulation of this argument see my chapter 'Tyranny as Demand', in Daniela Garofalo and David Sigler (eds.), *Lacan and Romanticism* (New York: SUNY Press, 2019), pp. 141–56.

noise that elicits mystery, motoring the narrative as it moves towards resolving the gap in knowledge produced by them. As Steven Connor puts it, 'Noise is anonymous, mechanical and meaningless; voice is personal, animate and expressive.'[44]

As has been established in studies of sonic Gothic by Van Elferen and others, since its inception, the Gothic has been a noisy business even if its soundworlds are complex and multifaceted. Atmospheric sound and noisy frights, perhaps the literary equivalent of what horror film critics term 'jump scares', that aim at generating Gothic affect are to be distinguished from auditory phenomena such as eerie or uncanny voices that are central to producing narrative effects. Matthew Gregory Lewis's Bleeding Nun is an example of the former: a noisy ghost producing affect but not sincere ethical effects. Through haunting the Castle of Lindenberg, the Bleeding Nun is the first ghost of the Gothic romance who haunts as a poltergeist and primarily through sound: 'till after her death She was never known to have existed. Then first did She think it necessary to make some noise in the world'. Taking-up the 'best room of the House' at Lindenberg, the Bleeding Nun rattles 'tables and chairs' by night. The soundscape of her haunting is replete with 'shrieking, howling, groaning, and swearing'; '[s]he wept and wailed... to the universal terror' of the Castle's 'Inhabitancies'.[45] In *A Sicilian Romance*, Radcliffe resolves the supernatural with a very real explanation of a tyrannical act. In Lewis, there is no rational resolution provided for this haunting. The Nun's reassembling of furniture by night, too, suggests that she foreshadows the poltergeist of the Victorian ghost story – even if it would be several years before Walter Scott would inaugurate the 'modern' ghostly tale in his 'The Tapestried Chamber' (1829), and even more time before the Victorian vogue for stories of seances cemented the poltergeist motif into the popular imagination.[46] In her appropriation from folklore and the oral tradition, Lewis's narrative of the Nun, which is recounted by Agnes de Medina to her lover Marquis Raymond de las Cisternas, provides an interesting meeting point between Victorian and Romantic auditory hauntings. The Bleeding Nun is primarily 'noisy', that is, unruly, an auditory haunting that seems unstructured and whose soundings, too, emphasise the polyvocality of even a single voice that can metamorphose into wailing, shrieking and crying. These seem to be *hysterical* noises and the gendering of the auditory is clear. Lewis deploys vococentric Gothic, then, to achieve rather crude effects, but

---

[44] Steven Connor, *Beyond Words: Sobs, Hums, Stutters and other Vocalizations* (London: Reaktion Books, 2014), p. 7.

[45] Matthew Gregory Lewis, *The Monk*, ed. Howard Anderson (Oxford: Oxford University Press, 2008), p. 139.

[46] 'Poltergeist' was not used in English letters until Catherine Crowe's study *The Night Side of Nature* (1848), even if the word was circulating in German-influenced culture in Britain from the 1830s onwards.

the hybridity of the Bleeding Nun's voice is an important precursor to what I term the 'monstrous' hybrid voice as it emerged in the nineteenth-century Gothic and beyond. I take up this aesthetic category again in Section 3's reading of the short fictions of Edgar Allan Poe.

2.1 Attentive Listening in the Gothic Romance

Such excessive and hybrid voices do not invite the kinds of attentive listening that shapes the soundworld of the Radcliffean Gothic and other Gothic mysteries of the Romantic period. Radcliffe's distinction between terror and horror in 'On the Supernatural in Poetry' is important to understanding the narrative and uncanny effects of vococentric Gothic. Terror, according to Radcliffe, 'expands the soul, and awakens the faculties to a high degree of life' while horror 'contracts, freezes, and nearly annihilates' the faculties. Thus, the model of attentive listening drawn from the writing of Angela Leighton, which I charted in Section 1, finds much resonance in the experience of the Radcliffean heroine who listens attentively to make sense of an auditory mystery, particularly if their visual sense is obscured by veils, mists or other atmospheric devices. Radcliffe concurs with the Burkean understanding that 'terror is a very high' source of the sublime',[47] but suspense can itself be pleasurable, activating desire and bringing with it the anticipation of an answer. This understanding of the attentive listener of the Gothic, who listens with the expectation of a revelation, has ramifications beyond Radcliffe's fiction; we can turn to the writing of William Godwin for another example of its importance.

Godwin's *Things as They Are; or, The Adventures of Caleb Williams* (1794) depicts two psychologically complex protagonists: the titular Caleb, who is an attentive listener and the first-person narrator of the novel, and his employer-cum-foe Ferdinando Falkland. In an early scene in Godwin's text, one which sets-up a mystery to be solved, Caleb hears Falkland sound a troubling note of unbearable 'anguish':

> As I opened the door, I heard at the same instant a deep groan expressive of intolerable anguish. The sound of the door in opening seemed to alarm the person within; I heard the lid of a trunk hastily shut, and the noise as of fastening a lock … at that moment a voice that seemed supernaturally tremendous exclaimed, Who is there? The voice was Mr Falkland's. The sound of it thrilled my very vitals.[48]

---

[47] Ann Radcliffe, 'On The Supernatural in Poetry', in E. J. Clery and Roberts Miles (eds.), *Gothic Documents, A Sourcebook, 1700–1820* (Manchester: Manchester University Press, 2000), pp. 163–72. (p. 168).

[48] William Godwin, *Caleb Williams*, ed. David McCracken (Oxford: Oxford University Press, 1998), pp. 7–8.

Once more, a groan uttered for an obscured reason fuels and drives a desire for knowledge. Indeed, Caleb seems almost seduced by this voice. As we may expect, his discovery of Falkland's despair over the occluded contents of a 'trunk' does not immediately lead to the revelation of a secret. But the promise of a sublime revelation is produced by the very obscurity of what Caleb believes he could have witnessed. As Monika Fludernik puts it, 'the sublime does not merely correlate with vastness but is also, typically, evoked by obscurity and can therefore be associated with mystery and veiled power'.[49] Falkland, we discover, was a man once driven to the murder of his tyrannical neighbour Tyrrel; as the plot unfolds, Falkland's framing of Caleb for this murder illustrates his own propensity toward injustice. In Radcliffe's oeuvre, the perplexed visage of St Aubert, as witnessed by his daughter Emily in *The Mysteries of Udolpho* (1794), is the paradigmatic scene in which a gap in knowledge – in this case a destabilizing of the paternal signifier – opens up, leaving Emily in a state of crisis and self-doubt, and beginning the central mystery of the narrative that Emily eventually resolves after her father's death.[50] Published in the same year as Radcliffe's *Udolpho*, Godwin's novel engages with wider questions pertaining to societal justice after the French Revolution and the role that public oratory can take in achieving or indeed corrupting it. The gradual unveiling of its central mystery foregrounds the importance of individual voice – speaking 'truth' with our own voice and reading the veracity of the speech of others – to uncovering sides to tyranny that societal face and reputation keep hidden. Mark Crosby has noted of one of the many trial scenes in the novel that Caleb's testimony against Falkland emphasises 'Godwin's distrust of the civic function of oratory, particularly in a legal context,' while also achieving Godwin's 'primary aim of exposing aristocratic fraud'.[51] Uncovering such injustice takes attentive listening; one must be ready to hear the moments when voices of power stutter, revealing themselves to be fallible.

In its characterisation of tyrannical force as voice, *Caleb Williams* suggests that such powerful oration is not only excessive, operating beyond societal mores, but that whoever is addressed by it has a predisposition to obey. Falkland's voice is described as 'supernaturally tremendous'; its power to command *should* be enough to close, or seal, the gap in knowledge that Caleb's discovery of Falkland's pain has produced. It transpires that in his fits

[49] Monika Fludernik, 'William Godwin's *Caleb Williams*: The Tarnishing of the Sublime', *ELH* 68:4 (2001): 857–96 (p. 860).

[50] See Robert Miles, *Ann Radcliffe: The Great Enchantress* (Manchester: Manchester University Press, 1995), pp. 142–8.

[51] Mark Crosby, 'The Voice of Flattery vs Sober Truth: William Godwin, Thomas Erskine and the 1792 Trial of Thomas Paine for Sedition', *The Review of English Studies*, 62:253 (February 2011): 90–112 (p. 108).

of rage Falkland ventriloquises, at least in a metaphorical sense, the tyrannical voice of Tyrrel whom he murdered, the neighbour whose own duality is revealed in his speech and voice, which can 'transform from the pleasant to the terrible, and a quarrel of a straw immediately ensu[ing] with the first man whose face he did not like'.[52] In this soundworld of unruly orality, Caleb is in search of a voice that mirrors his own sensibility and ethics: 'the voice of no man upon earth echoed to the voice of my conscience .. ... To me the whole world was unhearing as the tempest, and as cold as the torpedo'.[53] Caleb comes to understand the power of his own voice as a medium of revelation and revenge (be that ethical or otherwise), a voice of justice, he believes, that can break the will of his pursuer. As he flees abroad, pursued by Falkland's agent Gines, Caleb comes to a realisation. He perceives himself as a threat to Falkland because he can 'tell a tale', one that the 'justice of the country shall hear' him speak in a sublime 'voice more fearful than thunder'.[54] Inarticulate voices, then, give way eventually to a voice that can narrativise injustice and articulate it with potentially revolutionary force. In his pledge to speak in a thunderous voice, Caleb appropriates the power of the tyrannical voice for his own purposes; this voice is passed from Tyrrel to Falkland and then finally to Caleb for its final revolution and revelation.

2.2 Seductive and Ventriloquial Voices

Vococentric Gothic, then, can be used for many purposes, not merely to terrify or horrify but also to persuade or seduce the reader. Often understood as her response to the excessive visual horrors of Lewis's *The Monk*, Ann Radcliffe's *The Italian* (1797) presents a sustained, nuanced and sonically complex representation of several of the important forms that Vococentric Gothic can take in the Romantic school of terror. This includes a recognition of the voice as an attractive object of seduction. Indeed, from its very opening pages, *The Italian* foregrounds its vococentric concerns in Radcliffe's attention to the 'sweetness and fine expression' of the melodious voice of her veiled heroine Ellena.[55] In typically Gothic fashion, Radcliffe's framing of her narrative creates a distance between her reader and her novel's setting. Yet, *The Italian*'s many representations of sonorous and persecutory voices assert their presence and mediate or even undo the distancing between reader and text that is achieved through

---

[52] Godwin, *Caleb Williams*, p. 18.   [53] Godwin, *Caleb Williams*, p. 308.

[54] Godwin, *Caleb Williams*, p. 314.

[55] Ann Radcliffe, *The Italian*, ed. Frederick Garber (Oxford: Oxford University Press, 1998), p. 5. For a reading of the sublime voices of the Gothic romance, see my article 'My Voice Shall Ring in Your Ears: The Acousmatic Voice and the Timbral Sublime in the Gothic Romance', *Horror Studies* 7:2 (2016): 173–88.

narrative framing and historical setting. At least in one respect, Radcliffe's representation of the melodious voice coheres with James Beattie's understanding of the aesthetic pleasure derived from the 'natural voice' as 'the foundation of all true music, and the most perfect of all musical instruments'.[56] Radcliffe's Vivaldi, however, does not merely derive what Beattie may term 'pleasure' from Ellena's voice; instead, her voice is a desirous love object that, in a moment of synecdoche, draws attention to the desirability of her whole body. In Charlotte Dacre's *Zofloya* (1806), to provide another example, the voice of Zofloya is a sensual object that, for Victoria, sounds 'like the sweet murmuring sound of an Æolian harp, swept by the breath of a zephyr'.[57] The pleasure derived from voices in the Gothic exceed Beattie's sense of the pleasurable voice but they do not always do so without warning and peril. The devilish Zofloya's voice is infernal, a dangerously libidinous object.

James Beattie had a particular distaste for unruly expressions of passion, lamenting, for instance, the 'preternatural screams' of the operatic voice, which he defines as 'inharmonious notes of every kind, which a good voice cannot utter without straining'. Such 'inharmonious' or atonal notes, according to Beattie, cannot yield pleasure in their listener. From the outset of his remarks on music, Beattie connects human mimicry to mimesis in art, and his language is often highly suggestive of ventriloquism:

> Man from his birth is prone to imitation, and takes a great pleasure in it . . . he learns, by imitating others, to speak, and walk, and do many other things equally requisite to life and happiness. Most of the sports of children are imitative, and many of them are dramatical. Mimickry [*sic*] occasions laughter; and a just imitation of life upon the stage is highly delightful to person of all ranks, conditions, and capacities.[58]

Beattie's allusion to mimicry on stage most likely refers to the dramas of his time. Nevertheless, by the late eighteenth century, ventriloquists were performing on the Georgian stage, and ventriloquism as *theatre* meets Beattie's definition of 'delightful' art. For the voice to be truly unruly, it must be unbound from the stage: a shout in the street or, as in the Gothic novel of the period, a spectral sounding that moves through public spheres and private lodgings. While we may need to attune our readerly ears carefully to uncover the importance of disembodied voices to the British Gothic romance, their centrality to the American Gothic is more immediately obvious and founded in the pleasure of

---

[56] James Beattie, *Essays on Poetry and Music, as they Affect the Mind*, 3rd ed. (London: E. and C. Dilly, 1779), p. 122.
[57] Charlotte Dacre, *Zofloya, or The Moor: A Romance of the Fifteenth Century*, ed. Adriana Craciun (Peterborough: Broadview Press, 1997), p. 165.
[58] Beattie, *Essays on Poetry and Music*, p. 113.

mimicry in Brockden Brown's *Wieland* and its accompanying fragment 'Memoirs of Carwin, the Biloquist' (1803–1805).

Drawing its narrator, Clara, in the mould of a Radcliffean heroine,[59] *Wieland* recasts the acoustic concerns of British Gothic in its nuanced representation of the 'thrown' or ventriloquised voice, as well as in the suggestion that the divine voice is a symptom of madness. Clara reflects upon the Gothic power of the voice to transgress spatial boundaries that were once thought secure: 'I had vainly thought that my safety could be sufficiently secured by doors and bars, but this [Carwin] is a foe from whose grasp no power of divinity can save me! His artifices will ever lay my fame and happiness at his mercy. How shall I counterwork his plots, or detect his coadjutor?'[60] For Clara to convince her brother and her friend Pleyel that Carwin has spoken with her voice would necessitate her account outweighing the 'testimony' of Pleyel's senses.[61] The voice is a marker of subjectivity, as Dolar has argued,[62] and it has to it a 'fingerprint' quality through which the self may find a narcissistic recognition of its imagined uniqueness. In the occluded interpersonal dynamics of *Wieland*, to recognise another's voice is to mark another subject as present, and it is in promoting such misrecognitions that Carwin puts biloquism to work. Carwin's vocality is staged as being both uncanny and awe-inspiring. Carwin's 'throwing' of his voice may very well be the catalyst that leads Wieland to madness, but it does not compel him to commit the atrocities that ensue. A different phenomenon, the voice that guides Wieland to murder is authoritarian and diabolical, at least in what it compels its auditor to do if not in how it is represented aesthetically. The 'divine' voice, then, is a hallucination *prompted* by Carwin's vocal dexterity. The act of biloquism may be rarely referred to but its importance to the American Gothic tradition is clear:[63] Various reputations of it can be read from Brockden Brown's novel to the fiction of Poe and beyond. In such instances, the voice becomes imbued with a supernatural character that is either emphasised or, as in Brockden Brown's novel, eventually explained away. The voices that Carwin

---

[59] Jeffery Andrew Weinstock, 'Gothic and the New American Republic, 1770–1800', in Dale Townshend and Glennis Byron (eds), *The Gothic World* (London: Routledge Books, 2014), pp. 27–37 (p.34).

[60] Charles Brockden Brown, *Wieland: or, The Transformation: An American Tale*, ed. Emory Elliott (Oxford: Oxford University Press, 1998), p. 102.

[61] Brockden Brown, *Wieland*, p. 102.

[62] See Malden Dolar, 'Preface: Is There a Voice in the Text?' in Jorge Sacido-Romeo and Sylvia Mieszkowski (eds.), *Sound Effects: the Object Voice in Fiction* (Leiden: Brill Rodopi, 2015), pp. 11–20.

[63] The term 'biloquist' remains idiosyncratic – the entry for it in the *Oxford English Dictionary* is brief and proffers a short, straightforward and unambiguous definition: 'One who can speak with two different voices.' ('biloquist', n. *OED* 2021. www.oed.com/ [last accessed 13 June 2021].

produces may seem supernatural when they are executed, but a rational explanation is provided as to their source: his locutionary skill.

As Barbara Judson has argued, even in this early American Gothic text, the representation of internal and external voices suggests 'the eruption of the unconscious through an uncanny vocal economy based on ventriloquism'.[64] Judson's reference to the unconscious draws us towards considering the voice's formal and atavistic elements (timbre, grain, range) that resist symbolization. Indeed, the narrative voice of the Gothic memoir seems haunted by these constituent parts of the object, or spoken, voice itself. This dynamic is confirmed in James Hogg's *The Private Memoirs & Confessions of a Justified Sinner* (1824). Hogg is often described as using the conceit of ventriloquism and voice throwing in his narratives; David Stewart points out that Hogg clearly knew the ventriloquist Alexandre Vattemare, with whom Sir Walter Scott (Figure 1) was also acquainted. Indeed, Hogg recounts a humorous incident with Vattermare in a sketch entitled 'Scottish Haymakers' (1834).[65] Unlike Brocken Brown, Hogg does not present us with imaginings of 'literal' acts of ventriloquism in his fiction. Instead, his representation of the infernal voice is close to the monstrous hybrids that follow in the ventriloquial fictions of Poe, as is audible in Robert Wringham's description of Gil-Martin in *Confessions of a Justified Sinner*:

> when the being spoke, both my mental and bodily frame received another shock more terrible than the first, for it was the voice of the great personage I had so long denominated my friend . . .. I can scarce conceive it possible that any earthly sounds could be so discordant, so repulsive to every feeling of a human soul, as the tones of the voice that grated on my ear at that moment. They were the sounds of the pit, wheezed through a grated cranny, or seemed so to my distempered imagination.[66]

The discordant soundscape of this vococentric scene of horror clearly situates the infernal voice as monstrous, emerging as it does from a 'pit' of despair and hellish vengeance. Hogg's text intensifies the effect of horror in its positioning of an irresolvable uncertainty around the nature of the voice; is it Wringham's hallucination or is he really, like the victims of Maturin's Melmoth, being pursued by the devil? Just as the status of the voice intervenes in debates about the threshold between the internal, psychic world and the external public

---

[64] Barbara Judson, 'A Sound of Voices: The Ventriloquial Uncanny in *Wieland* and *Prometheus Unbound*', *Eighteenth-Century Studies* 44:1 (2010): 21–37, (p.22).

[65] David Stewart, 'Genuine Border Stories: James Hogg, Fiction and Mobility in the 1830s', *The Yearbook of English Studies* 48 (2018): 82–100, (p. 96).

[66] James Hogg, *The Private Memoirs & Confessions of a Justified Sinner* (London: Vintage, 2010), p. 175.

Walter Scott.

Figure 1 'Illustration of Sir Walter Scott, 1st Baronet FRSE
(15 August 1771–21 September 1832)': Getty Images
Source: Nastasic / DigitalVision Vectors, via Getty Images

sphere – where the voice may mark subjectivity and social certainty – so, too, does the ventriloquial voice become an important object of discussion in contemporaneous debates about the veracity of supernatural experience.

In his *Letters on Demonology and Witchcraft* (1830), which forms part of 'a series of treatises seeking to reconcile accounts of paranormal activity with scientific principles' published by Edinburgh-based thinkers during the period,[67] Scott

---

[67] Ian Duncan, 'Scott's Ghost-Seeing', *Gothic Studies* 24:1 (2022): 44–56, (p. 45).

connects questions around the unreliability of hearing to the performance of ventriloquism. As with Brockden Brown's fiction, Scott's writing on aesthetics shows a clear understanding of the Gothic potential of distance voice throwing, and the connected questions the practice raises around truth, belief and perception. Scott suggests that 'to the auricular deceptions practiced by the means of ventriloquism or otherwise, may be traced many of the most successful impostures which credulity has received as supernatural communications'.[68] These 'impostures' of the ventriloquist recall an important ethical dimension explored in Gothic narratives of the explained supernatural, such as Radcliffe's or Brockden Brown's. Particularly in Radcliffe's fiction, it is the inner voice of the heroine that must satisfy itself that what is told to them is truthful. The literal validation of finding the source of a disembodied voice in the Gothic (such as the quest for the source of the mysterious wailing of *A Sicilian Romance*) is part of a spectrum of voice investigations that includes a more figurative dimension: does a voice come from a deceptive foe, or a truthful friend? As mentioned in Section 1, Scott's letters would elicit a response from David Brewster, whose own work emphasises the enjoyment that may be produced in the misrecognition of the ventriloquist's voice. In contrast, Scott's *Letters* provide a treatise on the dangers of relying purely upon the 'auricular' sense.

For Scott, a 'whole class of superstitious observances arise, and are grounded upon inaccurate and imperfect hearing'.[69] In exemplifying his argument, he refers to wraith voices, as told in Hebridean myth, that are visitants said to forewarn of their own or their listener's death. These are ghost voices that Scott connects to oral traditions if only to contrast such forms with modern, enlightened thinking. In Scott's historical Gothic novel *The Monastery: A Romance* (1820), we are provided with a clear example of the differentiation that Scott makes in his fiction between human phantoms that are more modern, in spite of his fiction's historical settings, and the medieval magical beings that, as Duncan has put it, have 'no human original'.[70] In *The Monastery*, Scott's magical 'White Lady of Avenel' is a musical sprite who is able to influence and enchant the living with an infernal song: one monk of the monastery is told by his Abbot to 'say thy prayers, compose thyself, and banish that foolish chant from thy mind; – it is but a deception of the devil's'.[71] Acting as a counterpoint to the 'White Lady', Scott develops the motif of the wraith in *The Monastery* through the returns of Blind Alice, a mute visitant who appears but cannot communicate; for Duncan, Scott's modern phantoms

---

[68] Sir Walter Scott, *Letters on Demonology and Witchcraft* (London: Routledge, 1887), pp. 42–3.
[69] Scott, *Letters on Demonology*, p. 40.   [70] Duncan, 'Scott's Ghost-Seeing', p. 50.
[71] Sir Walter Scott, *The Monastery* in *The Waverley Novels: Abbotsford Edition*, 12 vols (Philadelphia: J. B. Lippincott, 1877), vol. 5, pp. 5–264 (p. 67).

'appear and, enigmatically, signify – portents communicating interpretive uncertainty – but they do not, cannot, *act* – exert physical force in the world, become material causes'.[72] In spite of such representations of aphonia, the musicality of Scott's spirits is one of their signature traits, and he is an important figure in the Gothic soundworld. *The Bride of Lammermoor* (1819) has been adapted countless times, perhaps most notably to opera in Gaetano Donizetti's romanticization of Scott's tale *Lucia di Lammermoor* (1835), while Scott's modern ghost stories would be hugely influential upon the development of the Victorian ghost story as a short story form.

Emerging from oral traditions, and associated throughout the Victorian period with recitals and 'fireside' performances, the ghost story as short story's genesis can be traced back to the German tradition, most notably E.T.A. Hoffmann's *Night Stories* (1817), which include 'The Sandman' (1816). In English language Gothic, we might position Washington Irving's 'Sleepy Hollow' (1820) and, as I mentioned above, Scott's 'The Tapestried Chamber' (1828) as proto-ghost stories. Matthew Gregory Lewis's embedded tale of the Bleeding Nun in *The Monk*, can be regarded, too, as an influential example of auditory haunting and poltergeist activity that shares certain motifs with some of the soundworlds that we find in the Victorian tale. To date, studies of the acoustics of the Victorian Gothic have produced only limited accounts of connections to the earlier Gothic romance. Kristie A. Schlauraff, for instance, recognises the 'echoes' between the two modes, while maintaining that listening to the Victorian Gothic 'demand[s] a distinct set of listening practices inseparable from the scientific spirit of the age'.[73] Yet, Matthew Gregory Lewis hears poltergeist activity well before the Victorian writers who would follow him. While the vococentric Gothic soundworld of dark Romanticism would prove to be extremely influential upon the acoustics of nineteenth-century horrors and hauntings, the writing of Edgar Allan Poe would produce monstrous, hybrid voices with a consistency hitherto not achieved by his Romantic precursors in the anglophone tradition.

3 From the Ventriloquial to the Monstrous Voice in the Nineteenth-Century Gothic of Dickens and Poe

The birth of the monstrous voice does not share its history or scene of genesis with the birth of the Gothic monster. In Mary Shelley's *Frankenstein* (1818/31), the creature is impossibly articulate and eloquent in its speech. Such verbal proficiency and skill is illustrated in its conversing with the blind Monsieur De Lacey and in the language it draws from reading Milton, Plutarch and Goethe.

---

[72] Duncan, 'Scott's Ghost-Seeing', p. 51. [73] Schlauraff, 'Victorian Gothic Soundscapes', p. 6.

It is the creature's visage and, eventually, its murderous actions, that set the parameters of its monstrosity. Its voice, however, is lofty and articulate, even human. Mostrous voices, I suggest, emerge fully in the soundworld of the Gothic of the decades that follow the publication of Shelley's revised edition of *Frankenstein* in 1831. The monstrous voice may have its auditory precursors in the writing of Matthew Gregory Lewis and James Hogg, but it comes into its own in mid-to-late nineteenth-century Gothic writing, where we find its fullest hybrid form taking shape in the short stories of Edgar Allan Poe. Attracting the critical attention of Fred Botting, Charity McAdams and others, Poe's voco-centric soundworld is much read and considered in the field of sonic Gothic studies.[74] Yet, there is more to be said about Poe's influence upon subsequent vococentric Gothic horror, as is evident in his influence upon Robert Bloch, which I elaborate upon in Section 4. Like the monstrous body, the monstrous voice is a hybrid creature. One of its most distinctive features is its unruly multiplicity; one body produces not just multiple voices but a horrific cacophony of difference that suggests an auditory form of vivisection. The distinction between Gothic terror and horror, then, becomes more pronounced in the auditory realm of nineteenth-century fiction: vococentric horror producing monstrous and excessive voices, while the ghost stories of the period, including those by Charles Dickens that I read here, recast the obscure and uncanny voices of received Gothic terror fiction to produce ethical and technologised voices. Poe was a great admirer of Dickens's writing. His well-known acoustic poem 'The Raven' (1845) is considered to be inspired by Dickens's fictional writing of his own chatty pet raven, Grip, in *Barnaby Rudge* (1841). The pair also exchanged letters in which they discussed William Godwin's compositional technique in *Caleb Williams*.[75] This shared interest in sound, however, does not produce wholly similar soundworlds in their mutual tales of the macabre, particularly in terms of voice.

3.1 Dickens's Ghost Voices

The auditory motifs that characterise Jacob Marley's spectral arrival in Dickens's *A Christmas Carol* (1843) clearly hark back to the noisy soundworld of the eighteenth-century Gothic romance. Attempting to exorcise a haunting before it even begins, Ebenezer Scrooge slams shut the door that holds the infamous knocker which transforms into the 'livid colour' of Marley's face.

---

[74] Fred Botting, 'Poe, Voice, and the Origin of Horror Fiction', pp. 73–100; Charity McAdams, *Poe and the Idea of Music: Failure, Transcendence, and Dark Romanticism* (Bethlehem, PA: Lehigh University Press, 2017).

[75] Fernando Galván, 'Plagiarism in Poe: Revisiting the Poe-Dickens Relationship', *The Edgar Allan Poe Review* 10:2 (2009): 11–24 (p.17).

The sound of the door closing, at least to Scrooge's heightened senses, rings through his home like 'thunder' and consumes the space of the quotidian: 'Every room above, and every cask in the wine-merchant's cellars below, appeared to have a separate peal of echoes of its own.'[76] The apparition's arrival, then, awakens a Gothic soundworld that signals a powerful restructuring of space, a world that Scrooge, at least at first, reasons against in spite of the ghostly phenomena his senses reveal to him. This heightening of atmosphere and of the senses is sustained even after the last 'peals' of echo diminish. In the moments before Marley arrives, all the bells in the house ring, gradually getting louder, heralding a break between time as it is perceived subjectively and chronological time: the sounds 'might have lasted half a minute, or a minute, but it seemed an hour'.[77] Even in death, Marley's voice remains a reliable marker of his identity; it is more his message – the symbolic content of what he says – that disturbs the 'very marrow' of Scrooge's bones than it is the timbre or presentation of his voice.[78] Weighed down by the sins that he 'forged' in life, Marley (Figure 2) creates his own noise, dragging his chains and sounding a 'clanking' that sparks in Scrooge a moment of recognition; he remembers 'to have heard that ghosts in haunted houses were described as dragging chains'.[79] Myth made real, the visitant seems uncannily familiar to Scrooge – the encounter is strikingly new and yet its form is somehow half-remembered. In making noise, Marley pushes Scrooge towards admitting a belief in spectres, but Scrooge's greatest transformation, at least in this scene, comes when Marley unravels his bandages to reveal his decayed and grotesque mouth, his lower jaw dropping down 'upon his breast'.[80] The very possibility of the articulation of a naturalised voice is suddenly placed in question. Even the familiar voice becomes, to paraphrase Mladen Dolar, an effect without a correlate cause – how does a broken jaw produce a familiar voice?[81] Scrooge comes to believe in the reality of the apparition even as its supernatural machinery is emphasised.

Scrooge's ethics are not truly transformed, however, until he encounters the Ghost of Christmas Yet to Come: the fourth, silent phantom of Stave IV. This is an apparition that, while mute, can conjure an impossible voice. A harbinger of death, the phantom transports Scrooge to face the ultimate limit – his own corpse. In immense darkness, Scrooge struggles (or perhaps unconsciously refuses) to recognise that he now stands in his own bedroom and that the 'plundered and bereft, unwatched, unwept, uncared for' body is him.[82]

---

[76] Charles Dickens, *A Christmas Carol and Other Writings*, ed. Michael Slater (London: Penguin Books, 2003), p. 42.

[77] Dickens, *A Christmas Carol*, pp. 42, 44.   [78] Dickens, *A Christmas Carol*, p. 45.

[79] Dickens, *A Christmas Carol*, p. 44.   [80] Dickens, *A Christmas Carol*, p. 47.

[81] Dolar, *A Voice and Nothing More*, p. 70.   [82] Dickens, *A Christmas Carol*, p. 102.

Figure 2 'Marley's Ghost' by John Leech: Getty Images.
Source: duncan1890 / DigitalVision Vectors, via Getty Images

Looking upon the haphazardly covered corpse, Scrooge hears an invocation that crosses the threshold from exteriority to interiority, as 'no voice' tells him that Death cannot alter the 'loved, revered, and honoured' and use them for 'dread purposes'. The good will be spared the horror of being Death's possession. The Phantom's conjuring of a message without a voice profoundly alters Scrooge. The voice's impossibility is tempered by its connection to silent prayer, and its delivery of a familiar, if sociopolitically informed, Christian message – Death will have no 'dominion' over those who earn goodness through a generosity of spirit in life.[83] The spectral voices that Dickens conjures in *A Christmas Carol* are all performable by the natural voice. They are not represented as traumatised

---

[83] Dickens, *A Christmas Carol*, pp. 102–3.

or technologised; they can all be spoken and claimed by their author. John Picker notes that,

> A decade before the debut of the phonograph, Dickens had used his lecture circuit to perfect and maintain a technology of oral presence. The tours transformed him into a reproducing speech machine, as his perpetual need to repeat himself fed and appeared to sanction his audiences' incessant desire to hear the same old hits again and again – primarily *A Christmas Carol* . . ..[84]

The Victorian ghost story emerges, of course, from an oral tradition that is maintained in Dickens's performance of his spectres as a 'speech machine', where the intimacy of fireside ghost telling is transmuted into an impersonal recital. Testament both to its ingenuity and its practicality, Dickens's fiction can conjure an *impossible* voice that may still be articulated by human speech in the theatre of authorial performance.

In his reading of *Our Mutual Friend* (1864–65), Patrick O'Donnell goes as far as to suggest that 'ventriloquy' is the 'master trope' of Dickens's last published text, serving 'as a figure for Dickens' historic revision of the power and uses of voice in a novel which reflects the anxious recognition that the representation of a 'voice', in reading and writing, signifies the conversion of identity into a public spectacle'.[85] O'Donnell draws parallels between what he reads as Dickens's conflation of impersonation with ventriloquism and the writings of Dickens's contemporary George Smith, a prominent historian and publicist of ventriloquism. Smith worked with William Love, a skilled Victorian performer of distant-voice ventriloquism, and published many versions of his *Memoirs and Anecdotes of Mr Love* (1831). Reading Smith's expanded 1856 edition *Programme of the Entertainment: Preceded by Memoirs of Mr. Love, the Dramatic Polyphonist*, O'Donnell argues that Smith's reflections on the art form produce the very 'conditions' of a 'ventriloquistic aesthetic' that are related to figures of impersonation and polyphony presented in Dickens's later writing.[86] Much more recently, Christopher Pittard has made the case convincingly that the scenes of domestic reading presented in Henry Cockton's extraordinarily popular *The Life and Adventures of Valentine Vox, the Ventriloquist* not only open-up the space for mimicry to be understood as a subtle act of anarchy, but allow Valentine, who in the story remains hidden during his ventriloquist performances, more publicly to lay claim to his talents and material. In a similar vein, critics such as Ivan Kreilkamp have understood

[84] Picker, *Victorian Soundscapes*, p. 7.
[85] Patrick O'Donnell, '"A Speeches of Chaff": Ventriloquy and Expression in *Our Mutual Friend*', *Dickens Studies Annual* 19 (1990):247–79 (p. 249).
[86] O'Donnell, 'Ventriloquy and Expression', p. 251.

Dickens's readings as a means of asserting the author's sovereignty over his literary product.[87]

3.2 Dickens and the Technologised Voice

Dickens toured for many years but, as John Picker notes, one story he never performed was his most overt tale of spectral technologies, 'The Signal-Man' (1866).[88] Written as a response, perhaps as a writing or working through of personal trauma, to the Staplehurst train derailment of June 1865, 'The Signal-Man' appeared in the 1866 extra Christmas number of his periodical *All the Year Round* as part of a set of short stories entitled *Mugby Junction,* which included contributions by Amelia B. Edwards and others. Dickens was a passenger on the train as it left the tracks at Staplehurst; although physically unharmed by the derailment, he was certainly psychologically scarred, witnessing the deaths of several fellow passengers as he tended to the badly injured. After the accident, he reportedly suffered from aphonia for around a fortnight. A script was prepared for 'The Signal-Man' to be read as part of the *Mugby Junction* Christmas collaboration, but the performance did not materialise, and Dickens never laid claim to his most troubling of ghost stories in a public arena.

Dickens's vococentric Gothic produces particularly uncanny effects by exploiting the sensory deficit between hearing a voice and locating it in space. The first object that we encounter in 'The Signal-Man' is the narrator's voice – that is, his *actual* rather than narrating voice: 'Halloa! Below There!' is a refrain repeated throughout the tale to uncanny effect. Through a careful twinning of consciousnesses and perspective, the first lines of the narrative that follow are focalised not through the speaker but from the point of view of the titular signalman. The reader is decentred and hesitates as to who is speaking. This sense of mystery is mirrored in the narrator's own attitude to the strange, distant man he has encountered; he comes to be puzzled as to why the signalman assumes that the source of his voice is 'down the line', at the signalman's level, rather than from above, where the narrator is located.[89] The narrator's voice has been thrown along the railway line, creating a disjuncture between space and voice and suggesting the collapsing of fictive levels. In the story world, the air is alive with vibrations not just of voices but the 'violent pulsation' of passing trains and ringing telegraphic bells. The thunderous roar of a Gothic

[87] Christopher Pittard, 'V for Ventriloquism: Powers of Vocal Mimicry in Henry Cockton's *The Life and Adventures of Valentine Vox, the Ventriloquist'*, *19: Interdisciplinary Studies in the Long Nineteenth Century*, 24 (2017), pp. 24–5 https://19.bbk.ac.uk/article/id/1514/ [last accessed 3 July 2022]
[88] Picker, *Victorian Soundscapes*, p. 167, fn. 72.
[89] Charles Dickens, *Complete Ghost Stories* (Hertfordshire: Wordsworth Editions, 2009), p. 260.

soundworld, once attributed to infernal and impossible voices, is replaced by the sublime 'rush' of trains. As part of his duties, the signalman operates a 'telegraphic instrument' that is connected to a 'electronic bell' to alert him to new telegrams. The narrator notes that the signalman 'twice broke off' their conversations 'with a fallen colour' and 'turned his face towards the little bell when it did NOT ring'.[90] We are reminded, then, of the limitations of the range of human hearing. A spectral *unsound* disturbs the signalman that cannot be symbolised in the Gothic atmosphere of the story, other than through a series of vibrating silences. As Fred Botting has put it, 'unheard sound ... exists on a double plane of writing, where real and imaginary perceptions are generated, reversed and confounded'.[91] In 'The Signal-Man', Dickens's 'double' writing and vibratory atmosphere resonate with the fiction of Poe, but clearly Dickens has recast his own handling of the apparition; no verbal warning is produced by the mute spectre of the 'Signal-Man' and the potential for a transformative revelation – akin to those articulated in *A Christmas Carol* – seems to be cut off from the tale's outset.

To recognise that such absences can be felt and sensed is to be sensitive to a spectral presence that seems telegraphic and modern in nature. In an allusion to the Staplehurst derailment, the signalman is convinced that the apparition's appearance 'down the line' is a harbinger, having already foreshadowed both a 'memorable accident on this Line' and, in a separate incident, a woman's death in her compartment.[92] The narrator's psychologisation of the signalman's experiences here reach their limit and fail to explain away the strange vibrations and hauntings visited upon the line. The narrator suggests that the apparition's voice is merely a meeting of Gothic atmosphere and technologised space: 'As to an imaginary cry, ... do but listen for a moment to the wind in this unnatural valley while we speak so low, and to the wild harp it makes of the telegraph wires!' He then challenges the signalman's perception of hearing the spectre ring his electric bell, to which the following rebuttal is given:

> I have never confused the spectre's ring with the man's. The ghost's ring is
> a strange vibration in the bell that it derives from nothing else, and I have not
> asserted that the bell stirs to the eye. I don't wonder that you failed to hear it.
> But I heard it.[93]

This 'strange vibration' of unsound is accompanied by the spectre's appearance on the line. Rather than give ethical guidance, allowing the signalman to work with the message of the ghost, its demand operates outside of any workable

---

[90] Dickens, *Ghost Stories*, pp. 262–63.
[91] Fred Botting, 'Poe, Voice, and the Origin of Horror Fiction', p. 76.
[92] Dickens, *Ghost Stories*, p. 266.   [93] Dickens, *Ghost Stories*, pp. 265, 267.

ethical framework – all that is audible is a strange command that echoes the narrator's first words of the story: 'Below there! Look out! Look out!'. The apparition signals the inevitability of a tragedy to come; it seems to demand something of the signalman but he is not able to interpret and to *work* with that demand.

The next evening the signalman is dead. Inexplicably 'cut down by an engine', he becomes the victim prophesised in the apparition's final warning to him. As the narrator looks down on the scene, he witnesses the train driver who was involved in the accident doubling the actions the signalman had once ascribed to the apparition: 'his left sleeve across his eyes, passionately waving his right arm'. It transpires that the last words called out to the signalman, as the engine came upon him, also have a familiar ring: 'Below there! Look out! Look out! For God's sake clear the way!'[94] This echo of the apparition's warning is the final refrain of a spectral demand that passes between the narrator, the apparition, the signalman and the driver. In turn, each of these characters mouths this utterance, as if it were a contagion, creating an economy of doubling that is achieved through what we can term, following O'Donnell's reading of George Smith's writings, an aesthetics of ventriloquial voice throwing. Beginning with the narrator's spoken voice, Dickens's execution of a vococentric Gothic aesthetic connects all four characters through echoes of the same portentous speech act. The story's denouement reminds us that a voice needs an attentive listener. The signalman is unmoved by the last and most immediate of the warnings given by the driver, his mind irrevocably attuned to spectral frequencies that torment him but from which he cannot discern any guidance that could transform, or recast, his destiny. If *A Christmas Carol* presents its readers with a series of ethical apparitions, with whom Scrooge must work to transform his life, 'The Signal-Man', as a text borne in real tragedy, is more fatalistic: the spectral voice may warn but it can no longer transform what is fated to be. This tragic representation of the voice is a Gothic lament. The Gothic voice evokes most pity when its power to transform is stripped away.

3.3 Poe, Ventriloquism and the Birth of the Monstrous Voice

Returning to David Brewster's letters provides a further reminder of the supernatural connotations of ventriloquism:

> The ventriloquist ... has the supernatural always at his command. In the open fields as well as in the crowded city, in the private apartment as well as in the public hall, he can summon up innumerable spirits; and though the persons of

---
[94] Dickens, *Ghost Stories*, pp. 270–71.

his fictitious dialogue are not visible to the eye, yet they are unequivocally present to the imagination of his auditors, as if they had been shadowed forth in the silence of a spectral form.[95]

In the opening section to this study, I drew attention to a passage in *Letters on Natural Magic* that highlights the Abbé de la Chapelle's account of Saint-Gille's ghostly 'voice from above', an auditory trick of voice-throwing that compelled mourning monks to lay virtually prostrate on the floor, before gathering to chant *De Profundis* in dutiful piety. The chaos caused by Saint-Gille's trickery is partly attributable to the fact that it took place in public. His act of aural deception was not 'framed' as artifice in the way that nineteenth-century ventriloquists' theatrical shows would be. The imagery of Saint-Gille's story is emblematic of Gothic romance. In seeking an exemplary mid-nineteenth-century Gothic soundworld it is necessary that we relocate from the streets of a 'crowded city' to the 'private apartments' and Gothic houses of Edgar Allan Poe. Locating his vococentric Gothic at a tipping point where, at any moment, terror may escalate into horror, Poe's true importance to any Gothic history of the voice is found in his splicing together of different forms of voice within one speaker or creature. His short fiction presents us with a series of impossible voices that are central to his narratives' invocations of terror, horror and mystery.

As I suggest below, if Poe's voices of horror supernaturalise the ventriloquial voice, his detective fiction invokes associations of the supernatural only to naturalise them and explain them away. In 'The Murders in the Rue Morgue' (1841), a strange 'foreign' voice of a murderer is heard by many auditory – if not visual – witnesses to the crime.[96] The identity of this impossible voice, as we may expect in what is often hailed as the first detective fiction, is eventually solved by Poe's Dupin, who ascribes the voice correctly not to a foreigner but to an animal, an orangutan. The locating and naturalising of Carwin's voice in *Wieland* is mirrored in Poe's story: the source of the impossible voice is surprising but not supernatural. Although not a Gothic representation, per se, the primal soundings of the orangutan highlight the cryptographic nature of Poe's voices, which themselves act as auditory puzzles to be deciphered. How could the multiplicity of interpretations proffered by the 'ear-witnesses' of the story be produced by just one voice? The voice seems impossible until Dupin deduces a rational if extraordinary explanation. A vocal event that seems supernatural may be explained away as the result of natural vocal effects: voice throwing, oral agility and all the rest.

---

[95] David Brewster, *Letters on Natural Magic*, p.172.

[96] Edgar Allan Poe, *Selected Poetry and Tales*, ed. James M. Hutchisson (Peterborough: Broadview Press, 2012), pp. 266–68.

There is narrative resolution, too, in '"Thou Art the Man"', Poe's late detective story that is directly influenced by nineteenth-century ventriloquist stage shows. The story is centred around unravelling the 'Rattleborough enigma' – the question of how the cadaver of Barnabas Shuttleworthy sprung from a box of Chateau-Margaux wine to elicit the confession of his murderer Charles Goodfellow. Two forms of ventriloquism, the macabre and the mischievous, are intertwined in this tale. Drawing from Steven Connor's account of Alexandre Vattemare's perform-ances, Susan Elizabeth Sweeney has noted that the macabre box trick that forms the heart of the narrative action in '"Thou Art the Man"' is Poe's morbid reimagining of a 'stunt that originated with Vattemare', in which the ventriloquist would converse with an invented man in a box on stage: when the lid opened, a voice would emerge, only to be silenced once the lid was closed.[97] Such a 'conversation' is a burlesque version of the 'fictious dialogue' that Brewster identified in his *Letters on Natural Magic* as the signature motif of the ventriloquist. In typical fashion, the box trick executed by Poe's narrator unveils a 'putrid' body:

> I inserted a chisel, and giving it a few slight taps with a hammer, the top of the box flew suddenly off, and at the same instant, there sprang up into a sitting position, directly facing the host, the bruised, bloody, and nearly putrid corpse of the murdered Mr. Shuttleworthy himself. It gazed for a few seconds, fixedly and sorrowfully, with its decaying and lack-lustre eyes, full into the countenance of Mr. Goodfellow; uttered slowly, but clearly and impressively, the words – 'Thou art the man!'[98]

The revelation that Poe's narrator is not only the *textual* voice for the reader but that it is his speaking voice that emanates from the cadaver of this Gothic box trick – the most important intradiegetic and accusatory voicing of the story – highlights the difference between the *ambient* narrative voice, and the inclusion of an excessive, or seemingly supernatural, spoken voice.

As it speaks through the cadaver, the detective's voice in Poe's tale produces and elicits a questionable form of justice. There is no doubt that the voice accuses the correct man, Charlie Goodfellow, who 'rapidly and vehemently' goes on to give 'a detailed confession of the hideous crime' before he himself drops dead from shock and fright.[99] Yet, the means through which Poe's narrator catches his killer are beyond the everyday course of justice; they are excessive and perhaps even unjust. Like magic, the ventriloquised accusatory voice causes the death, or execution, of Goodfellow almost immediately. Goodfellow had framed Shuttleworthy's nephew Pennifeather for the crime. In this light, exchanging Goodfellow's life for Pennifeather's seems just

---

[97] Sweeney, 'Echoes of Ventriloquism', p. 144.   [98] Poe, *Selected Poetry and Tales*, p. 354.

[99] Poe, *Selected Poetry and Tales*, p. 355.

enough. Yet, the accusatory voice acts alone, beyond the formal mechanisms of the law, and the sentence it passes upon Goodfellow (which is his almost immediate death) is certainly beyond what we may expect of Rattleborough's judicial processes. For all the empirical reasoning the detective narrator brings to bear in creating the 'Rattleborough enigma' there is little doubt of his disgust at the social performativity of a man like Goodfellow, whose charm and charisma lead 'the good citizens of Rattleborough' to completely overlook his '*manoeuvring*'.[100] And it is this disgust that drives the narrator to go beyond the law and play the ventriloquial and gruesome trick that catches the killer. As in Dickens's 'The Signal-Man', Poe's vococentric Gothic doubles the voice – both narrative and spoken – to produce an uncanny effect that disturbs the fictive layers of the story, yet the naturalisation of the corpse's voice at the end of '"Thou Art the Man"' renders the story's conclusion one of bathos and anti-climax rather than producing a lingering sense of unease. The corpse may be a horrific object, but the suggestion that it is being spoken through by our rather familiar narrator de-escalates any atmosphere of menace.

A century before the uncanny ventriloquist's dummy would emerge as a recurring motif of twentieth-century horror, nineteenth-century ventriloquists performed on stage to amuse and mystify their audiences using voice-throwing techniques without another body in sight. The performers' 'throwing' of voice emphasised the spatial deception involved. The disorientation, perhaps more pleasurable than truly terrifying, that audiences would experience in listening to such 'conversations' bear a resonance with the way in which, as I argued in Section 2, acousmatic voices of the Gothic romance are represented. Following Susan Sweeney's reading of Poe's voices, I use the term 'distance-ventriloquism' to distinguish the practices of showmen of the 1830s and 1840s from later ventriloquists who used dummies as conduits for voice. In the 1830s and '40s, the voices of Vattermare, William Edward Love and other performers 'appeared to come from inside boxes, behind screens, or offstage'.[101] As I established in the previous section, the desire to locate a voice – to put a face to it and ascribe its source – means that voice throwing is as much about deceiving the navigation processes of the ear as it is the eye. Poe was not only a reader, then, of Charles Brockden Brown but aware, too, of ventriloquist shows and particularly familiar with the distant-voice ventriloquist techniques of Signor Blitz who performed them in Philadelphia.

3.4 Poe's Soundworld and Impossible Voices

In 'The Fall of the House of Usher' (1839), both Poe's narrator and the reader are left adrift in an ever-transforming and discordant soundworld. The range of

---

[100] Poe, *Selected Poetry and Tales*, p. 355.   [101] Sweeney, 'Echoes of Ventriloquism', p. 129.

effects that Roderick's voice produces seems excessive, almost queer, moving as they do from 'tremulous' hesitancy to 'guttural' utterance, that is, from the hysterical to the dangerously primal. Most disturbingly, Roderick's capacity to emit a 'hollow-sounding enunciation' recalls the deep and a-symbolic groans of the earlier Gothic romance, and suggests that we are reaching a limit at which voice and discourse can no longer shield us from death and from a hollow abyss without language. Any rest or recuperation for the narrator and guest of Poe's tale is tempered by Roderick's predilection for the 'peculiar sounds' of 'string instruments' that create an uncanny and sparse soundworld.[102] The mentioning of 'strings' may suggest the a-tonal sounding of a violin, but in fact Poe refers here to Roderick's idiosyncratic strumming of his 'speaking guitar'. One connotation of this rich musical phrase is that Roderick's unsettling voice has been thrown into his instrument. The music of Roderick's 'speaking guitar' seems *beyond* true symbolisation in language or musical notation, and it is just such an inscrutable dimension that produces a sense of the uncanny. Roderick performs ballads for his guest – we presume singing while playing his 'speaking' instrument – and the words of one, 'The Haunted Palace', are transcribed in the story. Charity McAdams has noted Poe's resistance to describing this somewhat formulaic haunted piece as 'song'; instead, we are invited to read its lines as 'verses' printed 'without musical score'.[103] The embedding of the ballad's lines into Poe's short story is an act of ekphrasis but one that, although auditory in spirit, seems strangely mute as we traverse each verse. The poem does not sound as we may expect. A 'troop of Echoes', which once promised praise, has metamorphosed into 'evil things' that penetrate through the Palace's doors – the death of these echoes suggesting that voice in the ballad will no longer produce a song of vanity or narcissism; instead, the 'discordant melody' of the house of Usher seeps into the Palace and place of the poem, animating fantastical shapes, a 'throng' who 'laugh' but no longer smile.[104] It is hard to imagine what shape a face that laughs without smiling would take, the image perhaps recalling the sealed but mischievous mouth of the ventriloquist. The voices of Poe's tales seem rarely to be fixed – and they have very few foundations they cannot cast off.

In 'The Facts in the Case of M. Valdemar' (1845), the limits of how language can report voice are demonstrated once more but with one central contradiction foregrounded: the facts, mentioned in the title, seem themselves to be

---

[102] For a discussion of Poe's foreshadowing of the uncanny elements of sound and doubling articulated by Sigmund Freud, see Botting, 'Poe, Voice and the Origin of Horror Fiction', pp. 77–9.

[103] Charity McAdams, *Poe and the Idea of Music*, loc. 763.

[104] Poe, *Selected Poetry and Tales*, p. 197.

impossible and to belong more to the realm of the fantastic than to the reality that governs the world of Poe's detective stories. As Adam Frank has suggested, P–'s factual first-person narration mimics publications of the time that regarded the study of mesmerism as a scientific pursuit.[105] Valdemar's crawling yet cadaverous flesh, which ultimately produces his voice, is reported in gruesome detail: 'The upper lip ... writhed itself away from the teeth, which it had previously covered completely; while the lower jaw fell with an audible jerk, leaving the mouth widely extended, and disclosing in full view the swollen and blackened tongue.'[106] Yet, much of the form and sound of Valdemar's impossible voice that emerges from the dead, 'motionless jaw' of its enunciator escapes reporting: 'the hideous whole is indescribable, for the simple reason that no similar sounds have ever jarred upon the ear of humanity.' Reflecting the vast depths suggested by his name,[107] Valdemar is a vocalic space-producing machine, his dead mouth acting as a gateway into pits and caverns:

> There were two particulars, nevertheless, which I thought then, and still think, might fairly be stated as characteristic of the intonation . . . . In the first place, the voice seemed to reach our ears – at least mine – from a vast distance, or from some deep cavern within the earth. In the second place, it impressed me (I fear, indeed, that it will be impossible to make myself comprehended) as gelatinous or glutinous matters impress the sense of touch.[108]

Poe's narrator signals to us two signature qualities of the voice that Gothic writing habitually throws into relief. Recalling the subterranean vaults of the first-wave Gothic novel, M. Valdemar's death gasps conjure a cavernous space from the rather dim room in which he lays mesmerised. Gothic voice is powerfully synaesthetic and, here, 'glutinous'. In this acute multisensory experience, we are reminded of Usher's 'morbid acuteness of the senses', with the heightening of the senses that Poe achieves here escalated not to revelation but to a synaesthetic horror produced by the voice's body – its articulatory phonetics – coupled with the symbolic content of Valdemar infamous revelation: 'I am dead'. For Fred Botting, Poe's story may mark the birth of horror fiction itself, where the 'surplus effects of voice' move beyond uncanny registers by forcing 'an irreversible collapse of all bodies and categories'.[109] The absence of a clear cause-and-effect route between an articulating mouth and the production of Valdemar's voice suggests that monstrous ventriloquial effects are at play.

---

[105] Adam Frank, 'Valdemar's Tongue, Poe's Telegraphy', *ELH* 72:3 (2005): 635–62 (p.651).

[106] Poe, *Selected Poetry and Tales*, p. 369.

[107] Roland Barthes, 'Textual analysis of a Tale by Edgar Poe', *Poe Studies (1971–1985)* 10:1 (1971): 1–12 (p.4).

[108] Poe, *Selected Poetry and Tales*, p. 369.

[109] Botting, 'Poe, Voice and the Origin of Horror Fiction', p. 98.

But what about the hybridity of the monstrous voice that would become a hallmark of vococentric Gothic horror? In another of Poe's unsettling representation of the impossible voice, we encounter a polyvocality that is an example of auditory vivisection and an assemblage of noise. In 'The Black Cat' (1843), a monstrous scream reveals the burial place of the corpse of the narrator's wife:

> one long, loud, and continuous scream, utterly anomalous and inhuman – a howl – a wailing shriek, half of horror and half of triumph, such as might have arisen only out of hell, conjointly from the throats of the damned in their agony and of the demons that exult in damnation.[110]

The infernal voice is made monstrous; it emanates (impossibly) from the uncanny double of the narrator's cat Pluto whom he hanged and murdered. The monstrous voice is a composite of human, animal and even technological or mechanised sounds. Unlike Lewis's representation of the unruly noise of the Bleeding Nun, Poe's handling of the voice as multiplicity is refined, and carefully constructed to raise typically Gothic questions around the impermanence of the self, where any supposed boundary between the living and the dead might lie and just how porous it might be. The very *existence* of the voice as multiplicity often appears in his narrative discourse as an elaborate mystery, the source of which is either resolved as natural, as in his detective fiction, or that leaves an irresolvable sense of alterity with the reader that lingers even after the story's narrative action has ended. An important contemporaneous influence upon Poe's staging of the voice is to be found not just in literary accounts of ventriloquism but also in ventriloquist acts. Even with its recognised status as stage craft, the supernatural associations of the 'natural magic' of voice imitation never leave ventriloquism, and it is this tension between the real and the supernatural that many of Poe's vococentric stories exploit.

Poe and Dickens both provide a mob of impossible voices, be they telegraphic, ethical, monstrous or even, eventually, explicable as natural. The groans and melodious voices of the eighteenth-century Gothic romance give way to a modern spectrum of vocality informed by accounts of mesmerism and spectral technologies. Uncanny and monstrous voices sound through the quotidian amidst a nineteenth-century aural culture of vocal public performance. The influence of the Romantic Gothic, particularly that of Brockden Brown's Carwin upon Poe, cannot, however, be overlooked as we account for these representations not merely as reflections of their cultures of production but, too, as inheritors of a vococentric Gothic mode that had earned its spurs in the decades before Dickens and Poe were writing. When we think of the monstrous voice as hybrid and as multiple, we should not overlook the descriptions of ventriloquial acts that emphasise this

---

[110] Poe, *Selected Poetry and Tales*, p. 324.

multiplicity in the early nineteenth century, such as Scott's representation of Vattemare's art. On meeting with his friend at Abbotsford in 1824, Scott produced a dedicatory epigram entitled 'To Monsieur Alexandre' (1824) that characterises Vattemare as devilishly deceptive – 'Of yore, in Old England, it was not thought good/ To carry two visages under one hood' – and as a multiplicity:

> But I think you're a troop – an assemblage – a mob –
> And that I, as the Sheriff, must take up the job;
> And instead of rehearsing your wonders in verse!
> Must read you the Riot Act, and bid you disperse![111]

For all the joviality and good humour of Scott's verse there is a recognition that a writer like Scott, who had little time for modern ghosts and ghouls, felt compelled to police the decentring effects of the ventriloquial voice. Poe's association of such voices with criminality and madness, which he in part drew from Brockden Brown before him, would have lasting influence upon the figures of possession, be they psychologised or demonic, that would bring monstrous voices into the intermedial forms of twentieth-century Gothic horror.

4 Vococentric Horror: *Psycho*-Analysis and the Intermedial Monstrous Voice

Elaborating upon the definition of the 'monstrous' voice advanced in this volume so far, this section argues that new connections between the Gothic novel and the 'acousmatic' voice in film come to light when reading Robert Bloch's *Psycho* (1959), and Hitchcock's subsequent adaptation of the text, as the inheritors of a tradition of Gothicised representations of ventriloquism. It then reads Bob Clark's *Black Christmas* (1974) to demonstrate the influence that Bloch and Hitchcock's presentations of the monstrous voice has had upon horror cinema more broadly, as well as to further explore the ways in which the monstrous voice is connected to the murderous gaze. While Bloch's novel has received some critical attention from Gothic scholars,[112] there has been a good deal more interdisciplinary attention paid to the soundscapes of Hitchcock's *Psycho* (1960). Musicologists have noted the important sonic cues of Joseph Stefano's screenplay to the film and,[113] in a series of readings that pay sustained

[111] Cited in Suzanne Nash, 'The Appearances of "Monsieur Alexandre" in Firestone Library', *The Princeton University Library Chronicle* 74:3 (Spring 2013): 281–319 (pp. 287–8).

[112] For instance, see David Punter, 'Robert Bloch's *Psycho*: Some Pathological Contexts', in Brian Docherty (ed.) *American Horror Fiction: From Brockden Brown to Stephen King* (The MacMillan Press: London, 1990), pp. 92–106.

[113] James Wierzbicki, '*Psycho*-Analysis: Form and Function in Bernard Herrmann's Music for Hitchcock's Masterpiece', in Philip Hayward (ed.), *Terror Tracks: Music, Sound and Horror Cinema* (London: Equinox Publishing 2009), pp. 14–46 (p. 18).

attention to orality and its relationship to the psychoanalytic subject, the Slovenian School of Lacanian Psychoanalysis has framed the 'acousmatic' sounds of Hitchcock's film as exemplary representations of the traumatising dimension to the 'object' voice.[114] Less has been said, however, about the influence that the literary Gothic has upon these stagings.

Indeed, reading Bloch's *Psycho* alongside its first adaptation helps us to highlight a significant intermedial meeting point between the literary text, its filmic adaptation and its musical scoring. As Irina Rajewsky puts it, in its most fundamental guise 'the intermedial quality has to do with the way in which a media product comes into being, i.e., with the transformation of a given media product (a text, a film, etc.) or of its substratum into another medium'.[115] The intermedial 'coming into being' of Hitchcock's Norma Bates transforms her from an interior voice – the voice as delusion in Bloch's text, which readers at first assume to be *exterior* and audible – into an acousmatic, hybrid presence where 'the sound design of Mother's voice fractures the construction of subjectivity – she speaks not with one voice, but three, and none of them belong to the actor on screen'.[116] While Bloch is rightly framed as an inheritor of the weird fictions of H. P. Lovecraft, with whom he shared a much-cited correspondence, my reading of *Psycho*'s soundworld emphasises his work's relationship to Edgar Allan Poe's vococentric soundworlds. Elaborating upon these insights, this section argues that the literary tradition of Gothic ventriloquism has been foundational to the sonic assaults of modern and contemporary horror beyond even *Psycho* itself. That is, it locates *Psycho* in a broader body of films whose soundworlds produce vococentric horror through representations of possession, such as Alberto Cavalcanti's 'The Ventriloquist's Dummy' sequence of Ealing Studio's anthology horror *Dead of Night* (1945). In Gothic horror, representations of possession suggest the possibility that the alien or 'other' constituents of the ventriloquised voice can usurp the sovereignty of the subject entirely.

4.1 Ventriloquism as Possession

Indeed, the most striking example of ventriloquism *as horror* in mid-twentieth century film is found in *Dead of Night* (1945). Steven Connor's and Mladen Dolar's influential studies of the voice each include an analysis of *Dead of Night*

---

[114] See Mladen Dolar, *A Voice and Nothing More*, pp. 66–68.
[115] Irina O. Rajewsky, 'Intermediality, Intertextuality, and Remediation: A Literary Perspective on Intermediality', *Intermédialités/Intermediality*, 6 (2005): 43–64 (p.44).
[116] Ross J. Fenimore, 'Voices that Lie Within: The Heard and Unheard in *Psycho*', in Neil Lerner (ed.), *Music in the Horror Film: Listening to Fear* (New York: Routledge, 2010). pp. 80–97 (p. 90).

and editions of both books carry a cover image of the puppet Hugo sitting with his ventriloquist, and supposed master, Maxwell Frere (Michael Redgrave). Steven Connor locates the film as part of a 'minor thread in the history of Gothic cinema' that has a 'preoccupation' with ventriloquism.[117] However, the story's relationship to *Psycho*, particularly through its sound design, makes it a significant part of an important strain of vococentric Gothic horror cinema: namely, possession films.

Cavalcanti's sequence is told in retrospect and forms part of a series of stories in *Dead of Night* that are connected by their tellers at the Foley retreat, a farmhouse that provides the setting for this classically Gothic framing narrative. From the outset of the 'The Ventriloquist's Dummy' sequence, there is a foreshadowing of Hugo's supernatural abilities, with the dummy introduced in the narrative frame as the 'ghost in the cupboard' of Dr Van Straaten, a psychiatrist who has attempted (and failed) to treat Maxwell Frere. Van Straaten frames his story as a tale of attempted murder and split personality: 'one of the most complete cases of dual identity in the history of science,' as he puts it.[118] Incited by Hugo, and seemingly driven by jealousy, Maxwell shoots and injures his fellow ventriloquist Sylvester Kee, raising questions about his sanity but also around the volition of his supposedly lifeless dummy. After his arrest, Frere refuses to be psychoanalysed and his madness resists any diagnosis. The case is patently beyond the ken of Van Straaten's psychological theories that strongly recall the psychoanalytic technique of Sigmund Freud. The excesses of the voice once more resist being rehabilitated by a master discourse and the sense of supernatural alterity attached to acts of ventriloquism takes precedence.

In the narrative's final scenes, we begin to understand that Hugo's dummy body is incidental and that he exists as pure voice in and through Maxwell. Most telling is the episode in which Hugo is brought to Maxwell's cell, veiled by a sheet and laid down on the prison bed. Gasping is audible as Maxwell realises that he will be reunited with his dummy. These aspirate sounds signal a perverse excitement where terror and a sexualised enjoyment intertwine. Maxwell's face moves as Hugo speaks, suggesting that he has control, but Hugo taunts his ventriloquist; he will need a new partner, and Sylvester Kee can fulfil that role once he recovers from his wound. Enraged at this betrayal, Maxwell suffocates Hugo (suggesting that the illusion Hugo has breath has somehow become real) while Van Straaten watches on in horror, calling to the absent prison guards to intervene, as if he were witnessing a real murder rather than the destruction of

---

[117] Connor, *Dumbstruck*, p. 411.

[118] *Dead of Night*, dirs. Alberto Cavalcanti, Charles Crichton, Basil Dearden and Robert Hamer (United Kingdom: Ealing Studios, 1945).

a mere dummy. Hugo's frenzied cries are penetrating; they end once his face is smashed to the prison floor by Maxwell. Yet, in the next and final scene, we find that Hugo lives on as pure voice through Maxwell – the ventriloquist has been 'emptied out' and Hugo has taken full possession of his body.[119] Sitting upright on a hospital bed, Maxwell has a drained and pallid complexion, and he looks close to death. In a close-up shot, his eyes suddenly come to life as he realises Kee has come to visit; as if it has possessed Maxwell, Hugo's voice then utters 'Why, hello Sylvester. I've been waiting for you,' before the film transitions back to the framing narrative at the Foley farmhouse.[120] The parallels between the final scene of Hitchcock's *Psycho*, in which Norman addresses the camera from a sanatorium with Norma's hybrid voice articulating his thoughts, and the scene of a hospitalised Frere being spoken through by his dummy are clear. Hitchcock's ending to *Psycho* combines elements of Bloch's text with *Dead of Night*'s *mise en scène* and vococentric sound design. Both Cavacanti and Hitchcock produce beings of pure voice.

4.2 Robert Bloch and the Returns of Poe

Critical studies of Robert Bloch's writing remain scant; certainly, we know that he considered, evaluated, and imagined what it would be like to resurrect Edgar Allan Poe. In Bloch's body of work there are two resurrections of Poe of note: one is imagined and the other collaborative. Taking the former, first, we find a representation of the reanimation, or resurrection, of Poe in the narrative climax of Bloch's 1951 tale 'The Man Who Collected Poe', which was first published in the American pulp magazine *Famous Fantastic Mysteries*. The unnamed narrator, whom we know to be a bibliophile, visits the house of his acquaintance Launcelot Canning in Maryland. Canning's family heritage connects him back to Baltimore in the 1830s through his grandfather, and both Canning and the narrator presume some 'relationship' between the older Canning and Poe; one that has led to the family being bequeathed a number of Poe heirlooms, including an original 1843 edition of *The Prose Romances of Edgar A. Poe*, which Bloch's narrator suggests was once a 'trifle' that has now swelled in value to be worth $50,000 to collectors. Even if the narrator has no time for the 'literary hero-worshipper or the scholarly collector as a type',[121] he is drawn to visit the collection, partly as Launcelot Canning has the remarkable appearance of a Poe protagonist, his pale parlour, voice and crumbling home embodying a Poe aesthetic. If the visual motifs of fandom seem somewhat

---

[119] Connor, *Dumbstruck*, p. 399.   [120] Cavalcanti et. al., *Dead of Night*.
[121] Robert Bloch, 'The Man Who Collected Poe', para 5, www.cthulhufiles.com/stories/bloch/bloch-the-man-who-collected-poe.html [last accessed 3 July 2022].

overdrawn, Bloch nevertheless shows remarkable control of the story's sound-world. In the opening sentence of the tale, just as in Poe's 'The Fall of the House of Usher', we are transported to a 'soundless day in the autumn of the year',[122] with Bloch creating a baseline atmosphere of soundlessness – which has more presence, perhaps, than *silence* – that allows the crescendo of noise at the story's end to sound even more strikingly. That the narrator feels a sense of déjà vu on approaching the house is a playful admission that Bloch lifts his opening almost directly from 'Usher', creating a sense of uncanny repetition from the outset and establishing a deep textual connection between the two writers. The subtle changes of wording he employs in his deviation from Poe, as Jeffrey Weinstock has argued, creates a 'superimposition' of Bloch's opening paragraphs upon Poe's original, leading to a palimpsestic re-writing and doubling of an archetypal Poe narrator.[123] Launcelot's social mask, if barely apparent at the outset of the tale, soon slips completely as his maniacal side is revealed. His obsession with Poe has pushed him beyond the limits of rationalism towards witchcraft, demonology and necromancy. It transpires that the Canning family had exhumed Poe's body and kept his coffin, complete with corpse, in a hidden room in their home's basement. At first refusing to believe the actuality of this resurrection, Bloch's narrator is soon convinced of it when he is given a glimpse of 'a lofty and enshrouded figure; a figure all too familiar, with pallid features, high, domed forehead, moustache set above a mouth'.[124] During the confession of his transgressions, Canning is said to be 'babbling' like a madman, and the more his mind unravels, the further he and the narrator descend into the basement, the greater the cacophony of sound becomes: 'I speak of Canning's screams, and of thunder loud enough to drown all sound. I speak of terror born of loathing and desperation enough to shatter all my sanity.'[125] Like the House of Usher, Canning's Gothic house is soon consumed by flames.

Before Canning's home is destroyed, and the story reaches its climax, there is a fascinating scene of literary forgery that foreshadows Bloch's second literary resurrection of Poe. Lancelot claims to have copies of Poe's unpublished and lost works; the narrator, at first, reads them in astonishment only to come to dismiss them as fakes when he notices that the 'curiously *unyellowed* paper' on which they are written bears 'a visible watermark; the name of a firm

[122] Bloch, 'The Man Who Collected Poe', para 1.
[123] Jeffrey Andrew Weinstock, 'Edgar Allan Poe and the Undeath of the Author', in Dennis R. Perry and Carl Hinckley Sederholm (eds.), *Adapting Poe: Re-Imaginings in Popular Culture* (New York: Palgrave Macmillan, 2012), pp. 13–29, (pp. 19–21).
[124] Bloch, 'The Man Who Collected Poe', para 103.
[125] Bloch, 'The Man Who Collected Poe', para 101.

of well-known modern stationers, and the date – 1949'.[126] It is impossible, surely, for the sloping letters of Poe's distinctive hand to appear on modern paper unless some dark magic is involved. Bloch himself would soon be tasked with writing one of Poe's last and unfinished works on modern paper. His second resurrection of Poe was published just two years after 'The Man Who Collected Poe'. *Horror in the Lighthouse* (1953/1969) appeared in *Fantastic* in 1953 and was reworked for publication in 1969. In short prefatory remarks that appear before the 1953 originate of the story, Bloch attributes its writing to a suggestion made by the Poe scholar Thomas Ollive Mabbott who, after reading 'The Man Who Collected Poe', wrote to Bloch and encouraged him to attempt to 'complete' Poe's 'The Light-House' fragment. The sound-world of the narrative that Bloch appended to Poe's short piece is, as we may anticipate of nautical Gothic horror, a 'cacophony' of soaring waves and wailing winds. Bloch takes the theme of isolation introduced in Poe's fragment to excesses of horror by fleshing out the (if only implied) interrogation of psychic and spoken voice that Poe had begun in 1849.

In Poe's unfinished narrative, the narrator suggests that he has spoken words aloud in his confinement, that he is talking to himself with only his dog, Neptune, for company: 'It is strange that I never observed, until this moment, how dreary a sound that word has – "alone"! I could half fancy there was some peculiarity in the echo of these cylindrical walls'.[127] Even in its brevity, Poe's last work sets-up a tension familiar to the American Gothic since *Wieland*, one that transgresses any illusion of a neat distinction between interior and spoken forms of voice. The narrator plays a typically double role in this Gothic scene of isolation; he is both speaker and auditor. Bloch elaborates upon this motif and his narrative confirms the utterance of 'alone'; in his hands, it evolves into a 'muffled booming echo' that 'reverberate[s] through the lonely light-house, its sepulchral accent intoning "Alone!" in answer'.[128]

The connotations suggested by the auditory motif of the echo resonate with the Gothic's preoccupation with the disembodied voice and with its recurring representations of spaces of ghostly entrapment, such as the subterranean vault, castle dungeons or isolated prison house. As Steven Connor puts it, the 'echoing voice is not a voice in space, it is a voice of space. The voice continually touches, comes back to itself, marking out a volume in space in the interval between emission and return.'[129] The setting of 'The Light-house' suggests not

---

[126] Bloch, 'The Man Who Collected Poe', para 82. Original emphasis.

[127] Robert Bloch and Edgar Allan Poe, 'The Light-House', in Charles G. Waugh, Martin Harry Greenberg and Jenny-Lynn Azarian (eds.), *Lighthouse Horrors: Tales of Adventure, Suspense, and the Supernatural* (Maine: Down East Books, 1993), pp. 153–68 (p. 154).

[128] Bloch and Poe, 'The Light-House', p. 161.   [129] Steven Connor, *Dumbstruck*, p. 38.

just an echo of stories past; its built architecture of circular construction produces voice echoes that are represented in the story itself. Mirroring Connor's conceptual understanding of ventriloquism, we might suggest that an echo in the Gothic can be figurative (i.e., intertextual) or literal (i.e., represented), and that Bloch's finishing of Poe's story embodies both positions: intertextual echoes of Poe, on the one hand, are an effect of continuing the narrative; on the other hand, representations of echoes as a vococentric Gothic motif abound within the text. As in 'The Man Who Collected Poe', then, such intertextual echoes of Poe are an explicit example of figurative ventriloquism as Connor defines it. In my reading of *Psycho* that follows, I suggest that Poe's influence infuses the vococentric soundworld of Bloch's texts and echoes across the novel's reinterpretation in film and film music by Alfred Hitchcock and Bernard Herrmann, respectively. Isabella van Elferen has characterised the echo as 'a sound [that] can survive its physical origin both in duration and reach ... a phantom doppelgänger of its former self, temporally removed from it and therefore fundamentally out of joint'. Through her invocation of the language of spectrality, as well as in her allusion to the hauntological theories of Jacques Derrida, Van Elferen here emphasises the disembodied side to the echoing voice, but acknowledges, too, that it is etched with intimations of corporeality: that is, its physical origin is still perceived in the auditory realm through vibrations produced by the body. Emphasising the production of Gothic terror, van Elferen goes on to observe that in 'view of the disembodiment ascribed to spectres it is not surprising that sound, and often echo, is a preferred medium for Gothic ghosts'.[130] The echoes of Poe that we find in Bloch's soundworld are more horrific; voiced by monstrous and hybrid voices, they signal madness and the collapsing of boundaries.

4.3 *Psycho*-Analysis

The publication of *Psycho* in 1959 is important to the history of modern horror as it identifies the monstrous not as something that threatens from without but as something that is produced from within. To understand the foundational importance of vococentric sound to the *Psycho* franchise, we may start by listening attentively to the first chapter of Bloch's novel and, indeed, its very first sentence: 'Norman Bates heard the noise and a shock went through him.'[131] If 'The Man Who Collected Poe' sets-up a 'soundless' atmosphere as its acoustic baseline, then *Psycho* immediately draws our attention to its potentially shocking soundworld, even if all that startles Norman is, in actuality, the sound

[130] Van Elferen, *Gothic Music*, p. 25.
[131] Robert Bloch, *Psycho* (London: Robert Hale, 2013), p. 3.

of rain rattling upon the pane of the window by which he sits. As Norman reads
from Victor W. Von Hagen's *The Realm of the Incas* (1957), he lingers upon
a passage of Von Hagen's anthropological study that details a gruesome warrior
ritual in which the body of a captured enemy is skinned to form a 'sound box',
so that when the stomach is beaten, 'throbbings' emerge out of a 'dead
throat'.[132] The approach of Norma Bates disturbs Norman from his vococentric
reading. In its attention to sound, and with the focalization of the scene being
strictly from Norman's perspective, the reader is primed to listen first, and to
consider visual phenomenon as secondary. Norman does not lift his eyes to see
his mother. He feels and hears her presence, most significantly through her
voice: 'the voice that drummed into his ears like that of the Inca corpse in the
book; the drum of the dead'.[133] Let us imagine for a second that we approach
this opening scene afresh, with all the innocence of a reader in 1959 and prior to
Hitchcock's adaptation. Norma is not just alive on the page; she is presented in
the narrative discourse as a character distinct from Norman. She is not an offstage voice, as in Hitchcock's adaptation, but instead a clearly felt presence –
her voice gives her a face and, importantly, a gaze: '"Don't you think I have
eyes? I can see what you've been doing." She was over at the window now,
staring out at the rain'. Recalling Poe's subtle clue in 'The Light-House' that the
narrator has uncannily spoken the word 'alone' aloud, there are clues that
Norma is in Norman's mind, but these would be difficult to decode on a first
reading; what son has not thought of their mother, 'God, could she read *his*
mind?'[134]

   That Norma Bates feels as 'real' to the reader as Norman reflects two truths
about reading that phenomenologically distinguish it from visual media: first,
inner thought can easily be represented as speech if our narrator *hears* and
reports it as such; secondly, dialogue gives a character face and subjectivity.
Even if, as in Norma's character in Bloch's *Psycho*, that very being is predicated
upon a hallucination that the reader is not able to yet decode. In the literary
Gothic, then, dialogue equates with subjectivity. Utterances, as they are represented in the literary aesthetic, do not always carry the mark of selfhood
associated with the voice; indeed, a cough, a stutter, an 'um' or a growl are all
interruptions of the (false) sense of coherent subjectivity created by dialogue.
As such, Bloch plays upon and exploits the assumption that dialogue, unless
commented upon or framed otherwise, represents presence and body. Norma's
presence is powerful *because* her speech has such rhetorical force upon her son;
her body is not described at all, and the reader barely notices. Hitchcock relies

---

[132] Bloch, *Psycho*, pp. 3–4.   [133] Bloch, *Psycho*, p. 8.
[134] Bloch, *Psycho*, pp. 6, 10; original emphasis.

famously on the sound design and staging of what Michel Chion refers to as the *acousmêtre* to give Norma presence – that is, an off-stage voice, the source of which is never exactly pinpointed,[135] and which intrudes into Norman's space of the Gothic house. Bloch's medium already allowed him, through dialogue without comment, to present two subjectivities without revealing they are housed in one mind. In this way, *Psycho*'s representation of inner and outer voices inverts Brockden Brown's choice in *Wieland* to explain away the impossible voice as a trick or as a symptom of religious fundamentalism. Maintaining the illusion of two sources is convincingly achieved in Bloch's literary aesthetic given that, to paraphrase the writings of Connor, voice acts as 'face' in the text, where dialogue is the primary marker of a character's subjectivity: 'face and voice come to represent the emergence or figuring out (*figura* = face) of form itself'.[136]

The voice in both of these versions of *Psycho* generates horror in moments when psychosis is presented as a form of radical possession and where language is completely controlled by the Other. Bloch's novel connects Norman's ventriloquism of his mother's voice to a grotesque, atavistic ritual. He identifies with the 'contorted mouth of the corpse' as it mirrors his own symbolic death as Norma speaks through him. The scenario of the (m)other/Other speaking through the subject – here Norman – brings to the fore the alterity of language itself and its relationship to the unconscious. As Ferdinand de Saussure suggested, language 'speaks us': it is a system to which the individual subject has to adapt and harness as they come into language and, indeed, come into being as a subject in and of the symbolic. In certain senses, we are all victims of language, as we use it to define ourselves even though it is a discourse that emanates from the Other. This understanding of the subject's often troubling relationship to language plays an important role in the work of Jacques Lacan. As a psychoanalyst who revisited and expanded upon Freudian thought through the linguistic theories of Saussure, Lacan was intrigued by the role of the unconscious in language's speaking of us. As Lionel Bailly has noted, language for Lacan is 'not a discourse that the Subject intends, but that it cannot help but produce; it is obvious in the unintended emergence of repressed signifiers, be they in slips of the tongue, dreams, or in pathological symptoms.'[137] Our own language, then, surprises us, and, from this perspective, we may read fictional

---

[135] According to Chion, 'The *acousmêtre* is this acousmatic character whose relationship to the screen involves a specific kind of ambiguity and oscillation …. We may define it as neither inside nor outside the image. It is not inside, because the image of the voice's source – the body, the mouth – is not included.' Michel Chion, *The Voice in Cinema*, p. 129.

[136] Steven Connor, *Beyond Words*, p. 7.

[137] Lionel Bailly, *Lacan: A Beginner's Guide* (London: Oneworld Publications, 2009), p. 66.

stagings of ventriloquism as foregrounding – as excess – the alienating effects of producing speech itself.

4.4 Gaze and Voice

Noting the lasting popularity of slashers films, Jack Morgan locates Hitchcock's *Psycho* (1960) at the centre of a 'popular cultural carnography', one that, spanning modern and contemporary cultures, has lasted decades and which can be considered as a 'visceral discourse of the terrifying, in which *Psycho* seems to have become the defining icon'.[138] In the popular imagination, the iconic images (and sounds) of *Psycho's* horror are produced by the synaesthetic assault of Alfred Hitchcock's famous shower scene. The slashing of Norman Bates's knife across the skin of Marion Crane is Hitchcock's and Joseph Stefano's invention; the murder scene of Bloch's Gothically informed thriller is, in comparison, relatively brief, and leads to Mary (as she is named in the original novel) being swiftly beheaded by Norman's blade. Bloch's Mary receives a witch's death, a sudden and ritualistic decapitation that, to paraphrase Bloch's prose, cuts off her screaming.[139] Hitchcock's Marion Crane, on the other hand, screams and screams; her cries are placed in frenzied dialogue with the sound of Bernard Herrmann's piercing strings. The voice's status as an excess beyond language – and as representing a pure, inhumane drive to destroy the other – is reflected in Herrmann's score. Even more so than Bloch's novel, the cinematic version of *Psycho* emphasises Norman's scopophilia and con-nects the excesses of Norman's gaze to the overpowering and impossible force of Norma's voice. The silent gaze is a precursor to the thunderous noise of 'screeching' strings and Marion's screams.

Touted as one of the first modern slasher films, Bob Clark's *Black Christmas* (1974) casts the atrocity of the murderous male gaze even more directly onto the hybrid object voice.[140] For Jacques Lacan, gaze and voice are two objects that are inextricably linked in the sense that they set the parameters and limits of the subject. In Lacanian thought, voice and gaze are part objects that, when encountered by the subject, beget trauma and an almost impossible exposure to what Lacan terms the Real. As Alice Lagaay suggests, 'gaze and voice have

---

[138] Jack Morgan, *The Biology of Horror: Gothic Literature and Film* (Carbondale: Southern Illinois University Press, 2002), pp. 20–1.

[139] Bloch, *Psycho*, p. 39.

[140] As Sara Constantineau has identified, Clark's film was extremely influential upon John Carpenter's *Halloween* (1978); they share similarities in style and camera work, with Clark even suggesting that he discussed a sequel to *Black Christmas* with Carpenter, which would be set on Halloween. See Sara Constantineau, 'Black Christmas: the slasher film was made in Canada', *CineAction*, 82–83 (2011): 58+. Gale General OneFile (last accessed 27 June 2022). https://link.gale.com/apps/doc/A248407241/ITOF?u=mmucal5&sid=oclc&xid=381e7a35.

a quasitranscendental status' for Lacan as 'they refer to the fundamental relation from outside (the other) to inside (the self), which in constituting the subject at the same time defines it as lack'.[141] Following Lacan, Dolar comments that the extrasymbolic side to the voice is 'against *logos*' and the 'radical alterity' of meaning making.[142] Steven Connor, although sceptical of psychoanalytic accounts of the voice, has recognised, too, that '[t]here seems no limit to the extremity of the violence that can be conjured up by the invisible voice, once freed from appearance or embodiment'.[143] The voices that echo throughout the pantheon of horror literature and film suggest that exposure to the alterity of our own voice is a form of violence in and of itself.

Clark's film presents us with the atrocities of the male gaze by channelling its essential violence into the auditory realm; that is, through a series of obscene telephone calls that are made to a sorority house by an anonymous murderer who is known as 'the moaner' or 'Billy' and whose identity is never revealed. After the film's opening credit sequence presents a portrait of the festively decorated sorority house, the camera quickly takes on the more subjectivised gaze of a peeping tom (most likely to be the killer's perspective) as it stalks around the perimeter of the house before moving *inside* into the attic. We hear heavy and laboured breathing: animalistic snarling that connotes an unruly and perverse desire. Clark's horror soundworld, then, is more visceral and guttural than the uncanny 'ghost noise' produced by more classically Gothic cinema.[144] The moaner's voice is both inside and outside the house – the 'calls are coming from inside the house' being a now cliched trope of horror film that *Black Christmas* inaugurates. It is through the telephone that the moaner makes most intimate contact with his victims-to-be. The phone's earpiece becomes a voice box, producing an array of animal and techonlogised oral sounds, from static interference to animal cries, to crackling and to obscene language. As the sorority sisters gather around the telephone (Figure 3) to listen communally to this bizarre, extrasymbolic ranting, it is at first treated as a performance that presents no immediate threat, the implication being that the bearer of the telephonic voice must be far away even if his voice can pass through their hallway from the earpiece.[145] The breath of the caller, though, cannot yet be felt down their necks. Connor has commented that 'all voice is shaped breath' but that 'articulation' into language (and therefore social discourses) involves a 'chivvying of the voice' to

---

[141] Alice Lagaay, 'Between Sound and Silence: Voice in the History of Psychoanalysis', *Episteme*, 1:1 (2008): 53–63 (p. 59).

[142] Dolar, *A Voice and Nothing More*, p. 52. Original emphasis.

[143] Connor, *Dumbstruck*, p. 405.

[144] For an enlightening discussion of 'ghost noise' in Golden Age Horror films of the 1930s, see Murray Leeder, *Horror Film: A Critical Introduction* (London: Bloomsbury, 2018), pp. 164–9.

[145] *Black Christmas*, dir. Bob Clark. (Canada: Canadian Film Development Corporation, 1974).

Figure 3 '*BLACK CHRISTMAS (1974) SILENT NIGHT, EVIL NIGHT: OLIVIA HUSSEY, MARGOT KIDDER*'.
Source: Moviestore Collection Ltd/Alamy Stock Photo.

form diction.[146] The moaner's voice is far too corporeal to suggest that any 'shaping' of breath has taken place; its alterity, too, disrupts modes of 'attentive' listening. The sorority girls listen carefully to the calls but can make no sense of them. There is no body visible; corporeality is audible only in its voice-traces.

The film's music carefully frames and supplements the moaner's voice, and the score's instrumentation is arranged around *Black Christmas*'s vococentric theme. The opening titles are accompanied by a rendition of Franz Xaver Gruber's popular Christmas carol 'Silent Night' (1818). As in Bloch's novel *Psycho*, then, we open with an invitation to listen and to attune our ears to silence to heighten our senses in preparation for a series of exposures to the monstrous voice. Midway through the film Peter Smythe (Keir Dullea), the suspicious-looking boyfriend of Jess Barnard (Olivia Hussey), gives a piano recital of an atonal and bruising modernist piece at his conservatoire, a composition which itself could soundtrack a horror film. Indeed, we might even suggest that in the film Peter's playing moves from being diegetic to non-diegetic. Discordant and fiercely struck piano chords later soundtrack the calls

---

[146] Steven Connor, 'Whisper Music', (2008). http://stevenconnor.com/whisper-music.html, para 1 [last accessed 3 July 2022].

from the moaner and echo Peter's discordant playing. Peter is clearly located as a suspect; his music seems to reflect his tortured soul. In a violent rage he damages the conservatoire's piano after his playing is deemed not sophisticated enough for his teachers. Peter's furious outburst in the recital room is mirrored just a few scenes later in Billy's destruction of a few heirlooms held in the sorority house's attic. Peter, though, is not the moaner nor is he a murderer. He is merely a tortured artist. While the film suggests, ultimately, that no one body can feasibly be the source of the impossible and hybrid voice that calls, its screenplay often draws parallels between some of the auditory and affective elements that combine to make the moaner's voice and the plight of characters in the film. After refusing a proposal from Peter, Jess Barnard is startled out of her contemplative mood by the sound of her sorority sister Barb Coard (Margot Kidder) gasping for breath in her bedroom. Jess discovers that Barb is having an asthma attack; the deep, rasping and constricted breaths that Barb forces out sound very much like they could form part of the moaner's hybrid and monstrous voice. Even if the moaner's voice seems an impossible one, it has certain dimensions (even beyond its ability to articulate speech) that suggest a connection to humanity and subjectivity. The monstrous voice, then, is thrown or doubled across the cast. Most human of all, the moaner's voice has a tragic element; it pleads for help on a number of occasions. The tragedy is that the moaner knows he cannot stop what is fated to be; he will kill again.

Steven Connor has argued that voices can 'themselves produce bodies'; these auditory yet corporeal phenomena may be unseen in the horrors that I have read in this section but their presences are certainly felt. The vocalic body becomes a screen onto which an array of horrors are projected, and such hybrid voices are the production, ultimately, of murderous rage. Cohering with Gothic motifs of doubling and of possession, Connor suggests that the voice, in its guise as an expression of pure anger, is ultimately at war with itself: 'the angry or demanding voice at once destroys and defends itself – in fact, defends itself against itself . . . the voice cracks with the effort to surpass its own condition, to become an action.'[147] The Gothic voices of horror crave to commit taboo acts, including murder and other depravities. In its focus upon adaptation and the intermedial monstrous voice, this section has recognised that monstrosity can present itself through violent voice. There are visual correlates to the horror of Norma's voice and the moaner's groaning, evident in the skeletal corpses or dead and violated bodies of these fictions. The hybridity of these voices, however, makes them distinctively more monstrous than what is presented visually. In *Dead of Night*, Hugo leaves his dummy body only to become more empowered as pure voice. These noisy voices are impossible because of their supernatural sources or their hybrid multiplicity.

---

[147] Connor, *Dumbstruck*, pp. 35, 37.

Silence, though, can also be considered a representation of the alterity of pure voice, and it is to the notion of the unrepresentable voice – the voice as a form of *unsound* – that I turn to in the next section's reading of *The Black Tapes* horror podcast.

5 Conclusion: The Gothic Echo Chamber and the Contemporary Horror Podcast

> Lucifer, now referred to as Satan in this particular gospel, created some kind of musical back door as he fell into the inferno. Something sonic that would allow Satan and his minions back into the world without God knowing. This mysterious note is apparently a sound that God can't hear. The Unsound.[148]

Wrapping windows, creaking floorboards, the groaning of disembodied voices and the distant cry of a heroine: these are just some of the inherited acoustic motifs that are reiterated throughout the Gothic's 'cross-platform' texts in contemporary media.[149] As we have seen, these motifs echo transhistorically with the voices and noise of vococentric Gothic first crying out in novel form in the eighteenth-century Gothic romance and reverberating across and through time into modern and contemporary film. Where auditory technological innovation occurs – the phonograph, the telephone – the Gothic follows, bringing with it a troop of uncanny and monstrous voices, which move through space, pulsing even through wires and telephone lines. Certainly, listening attentively to the Gothic leads us to encounter echoes of what went before, suggesting that while inherited modes of representation may be reformed to suit new media and new times, they are not wholly reinvented. The vococentric Gothic survives 'its physical origin both in duration and reach',[150] but technological interventions such as film sound design serve to create new aesthetic 'voicings' of these motifs. Where there are disembodied voices that cross boundaries, beckoning towards a revelation or the germ of a hidden secret, there is sound, too, which seems beyond the threshold of the audible: 'noises outside our range: those too high or too low for human detection, or just too far away'.[151] In examining the ways in which acoustic motifs sound (or *unsound*) in contemporary media this study closes with a reading of the mockumentary podcast *The Black Tapes* (2015–17). In the series, the unsound is suggested to be the devil's voice itself, with the augmented fifth or the devil's note (what the show terms '*diabolica lyricasis*') foregrounded (Sound 2). *The Black Tapes* wears its literary influences on its sleeve, and the unsound's status as an impossible object returns us to

---

[148] 'The Unsound', *The Black Tapes,* Episode 103 [Podcast] (Paul Bae and Terry Miles, 2015). http://theblacktapespodcast.com/?offset=1441746399343.

[149] Danielle Barrios-O'Neill, 'Editor's Introduction' to *Fearful Sounds: Cross-Platform Studies of Sonic Audio and Horror, Revenant* special issue 3 (2018): 1–4 (p. 1).

[150] Van Elferen, *Gothic Music*, p. 25.   [151] Leighton, *Hearing Things*, p. 22.

psychoanalytic accounts of the 'object' voice, which, as Slavoj Žižek argues, can find its ultimate expression in voicelessness and silence.[152]

Sound 2 'From *THE BLACK TAPES* PODCAST EPISODE 103'. Audio file available at www.cambridge.org/foley
Source: 'The Unsound', *The Black Tapes*, Episode 103 [Podcast] (Paul Bae and Terry Miles, 2015). Available Online: http://theblacktapespodcast.com/?offset=1441746399343.

5.1 Unsound and The Horror Podcast

Podcasting is a vococentric medium with the timbre of the voice its foundation. As Leslie Grace McMurtry has noted, the enduring cultural and critical questions around the status of auditory drama in relation to other art forms – its relationship to literature; its positioning as high or low culture – allows it to be a highly inventive mode,[153] one that can play with and transgress conventions as much as reiterate them in its many genre fictions. As with the act of reading, there is an intimacy to listening to audio drama that Gothic horror dramas exploit. Sound moves into and through us, effortlessly crossing the external/ internal divide through our aural sense. As Richard Hand highlights, 'horror audio often utilises subjective/objective mediation' creating 'a crossover between interior consciousness and external context'.[154] In spite of its disruption of spatial and critical boundaries, horror podcasting in the last few years has come to be defined and located by scholarship as a discrete genre if not industry of its own. *The Black Tapes* has already gained some scholarly attention among critics of Gothic audio drama and it, too, has an enduring appeal to its online fandom.[155] One reason why *The Black Tapes* keeps a sense of enigma in place across its episodes is that it is yet to formally end; its final episode, first broadcast in 2017, was renamed as a 'mid-season finale' on its re-release in 2020 but no subsequent episodes have followed. Not only, then, is there the silence surrounding the mysterious qualities of 'unsound' to consider, the series' disappearance from our Really Simple Syndication (RSS) feeds has

---

[152] Slavoj Žižek, '"I Hear You with My Eyes"; or, The Invisible Master', in Renata Salecl and Slavoj Žižek (eds.), *Gaze and Voice as Love Objects* (New York: Duke University Press, 1996), pp. 90–126.

[153] Leslie Grace McMurtry, *Revolution in the Echo Chamber: Audio Drama's Past, Present and Future* (Bristol: Intellect Books, 2019).

[154] Richard J. Hand, *Listen in Terror: British Horror Radio from the Advent of Broadcasting to the Digital Age* (Manchester: Manchester University Press, 2014), p. 201.

[155] See, for instance, Dannielle Hancock and Leslie McMurtry, '"Cycles upon cycles, stories upon stories": contemporary audio media and podcast horror's new frights', *Palgrave Communications 3*, 17075 (2017): https://doi.org/10.1057/palcomms.2017.75 [last accessed 3 July 2022].

created its own sense of cultural silence and lack among its dedicated followers, leaving many of the narrative mysteries raised by the show unanswered no matter how attentively we may listen for their resolution.

The podcast is differentiated from a radio broadcast not merely in the way it is packaged for its audience (as an episodic production) and distributed to them (via RSS feeds and audio streaming platforms). As I suggested above, critics also regard podcast listening to be a more *intimate* experience than the feeling of simultaneously connecting with other listeners that forms part of the audience experience in (live) broadcast radio. With this increased sense of intimacy, which Richard Berry has termed a 'hyper-intimacy',[156] the podcast listener takes on the position of a secret sharer and, once their defences are relaxed, the potential for an experience of aural horror is opened-up. Throughout this volume, I have emphasised that Gothic soundworlds render signature atmospheres, that Gothic horror exploits the penetrating attributes of sound and voice, and that that both are inherently spatial phenomenon. The intimate horror podcast exploits all these elements. As a post-*Serial* (2014–present) digital horror podcast, *The Black Tapes* reflects not only on its own medium, but also references its analogue precursors, most evident in its titular reference to the videotape. The Strand Institute's tapes are described across several passages of ekphrasis – that is, the listener only has access to spoken descriptions of these auditory-visual recordings.[157] Given the meta-attention to issues of hearing and sound that forms so much of the series' character, we may have expected these black tapes to be audio cassettes. The motif of the videotapes, however, makes a clear connection between this horror podcast and found footage cinema. Indeed, anyone with even a passing familiarity with Hideo Nakata's *Ringu* (1998) will recognise where one of *The Black Tapes*' central myths – that those who listen to the unsound will die within a year – finds its filmic root and parallel.

Sharing many of its defining narrative features with other examples of the horror podcast genre, *The Black Tapes* is an assemblage of Gothic tropes past that are infused and somewhat enlivened by the series' self-reflective nature and the intertextual soundworld it creates. As Hancock and McMurtry have put it, the horror podcast is 'a synthesized panorama of forms' and *The Black Tapes* is a standout example of the genre,[158] a series particularly cognisant of the limitations and possibilities that its form, and the way that it is consumed by a cult listenership, present. In the show, the American Weird's long-held fasciation for the 'inscrutable' other is transposed into an auditory spectre. As Hand has noted,

---

[156] See Richard Berry, 'Podcasting: Considering the evolution of the medium and its association with the word "radio"', *The Radio Journal International Studies in Broadcast and Audio Media*, 14:1 (2016), pp. 7–22.

[157] *The Black Tapes*, Episode 102.

[158] Hancock and McMurtry, 'Cycles upon Cycles', n.p. abstract.

'[h]orror audio … makes use of unnerving sound in its purest form: namely, through the scream and through silence.'[159] *The Black Tapes* presents us with an unsound that, if not silent, is indecipherable by its listener. The unsound is associated with music, both classical and contemporary, which suggests that it *generates* representation even as it resists it. In Episode 103, when we hear a version of the unsound that is represented as an a-tonal and technologised series of sounds, we sense that it is a modern and counterfeit version of another, more inscrutable and *mythic* unsound itself. Disseminated on Internet forums and the dark web, the audio file that contains the modern unsound arrives from unverifiable sources, and the original purpose of its recording is impossible to discern. If the true horror of the voice is found in its guttural and pre-symbolic elements, *The Black Tapes* recognises that a-symbolic sounds (which the counterfeit unsound resembles) are open to sublimation, and that their alienating effects can be remedied through post-symbolic means of representation, such as music. Such acts of diabolical sublimation are embodied by the character of Percival Black in the series: a Hoffmann-esque figure and devilish composer.[160] In Episode 109, it is suggested that Black's music may be the antidote to hearing the unsound, a way for its listener to escape their fated destiny of death.

As indicated in the epigraph to this section, in which Keith Dabic, the guitarist of fictional Seattle rock band 'Hastur Rising', describes its cult history, the unsound, then, is associated with the devil's music in the series. In addition, it is characterised as a vococentric Gothic motif. As implied by my reading of late eighteenth-century oralities in Section 2, the satanic voice is represented in the Gothic romance as negatively sublime, such as in Charles Maturin's *Melmoth the Wanderer*, or as a seductive object, such as in Charlotte Dacre's *Zofloya* or Matthew Gregory Lewis's *The Monk*. In *The Black Tapes*, however, the satanic voice is part of a mythic occulture that sketches out and recasts the conspiracy theories and mythic worlds that belong to the turn of the twentieth century. The extensive mythmaking involved in locating the unsound makes explicit reference to Aleister Crowley, H. P. Lovecraft, and The Hermetic Order of the Golden Dawn. Given that it is indecipherable but fascinating nevertheless, being exposed to the unsound engenders what S. T. Joshi would term an experience of pure Lovecraftian 'supernatural horror', that is, not just an experience of fear and disgust but 'the *contemplation* of something appalling and dreadful'.[161] If its modern incarnation can be heard and even dissected, then the very impossibility of encountering the mythic unsound connects it also to representations of noiselessness that have recurred throughout the history of

---

[159] Hand, *Listen in Terror*, p. 201.   [160] *The Black Tapes*, Episode 109.
[161] S. T. Joshi, *Unutterable Horror: A History of Supernatural Fictions*, 2 vols. (New York: Hippocampus Press, 2014), vol. 1, p. 9.

Gothic radio drama.[162] The appeal of this mythic motif is clear. There is a perverse and desirable enjoyment to be had in tracking down a secret sound that not even a divine Other can hear.

The mythic unnsound is a portal to unveiling a new world; hearing it, so the belief system surrounding it in *The Black Tapes* goes, would transform experience itself. As Dr Richard Strand, the shadowy scholar and paranormal investigator whose Institute acts as a gatekeeper for the black tapes, notes, the unsound is an invitation transmitted through pure voice, an 'archdemon . . . gently asking the listener to invite him into his world'.[163] The unsound is said to be a 'backdoor', a threshold through which we can pass to experience something radical. Yet, as *The Black Tapes* attests, there is an essence to the voice that escapes representations transmedially. As with the monstrous voices of horror film, unsound is a monstrous screen onto which many different cultural myths and phantoms are projected. In other words, unsound is a *vortex* around which discourses of alterity circulate but never reveal; its pervasive auditory traces remind us of Poe's and of Dickens's 'vibrations':[164] 'what you call the Unsound behaves very much like a low frequency wave. We're not supposed to be able to hear these frequencies, yet here it is, emitting an audible sound.'[165] Even when it is located as an inaudible 'wave', the unsound's orality is never far away. The series' 'structural acoustician' Professor Pullman suggests that the genesis of the modern unsound may be an 'organic' voice that has been transformed and technologised. His scientific investigation reveals, then, yet another Gothic threshold of listening that activates and engages its listeners' desire to *know*: to hear the voice that lies beneath the noise. Even where the modern unsound is presented as an unstructured series of indecipherable sounds on the threshold of being heard, the effects it produces remain those we associate with the hybrid and impossible voices of the Gothic. The unsound is an auditory object located between the natural and the supernatural, one that generates terror, horror and, above all, a sense of inscrutable mystery. It is a voice transformed.

5.2 Conclusion

'Between about 1750 and 1925', Jonathan Sterne argues, evolving methodologies of listening 'harnessed, modified, and shaped . . . powers of auditory perception in the service of rationality. In the modern age, sound and hearing were reconceptualized, objectified, imitated, transformed, reproduced, commodified, mass-produced, and industrialized.'[166] The soundworld of the

---

[162] Hand, *Listen in Terror*, p. 9.   [163] *The Black Tapes*, Episode 103.
[164] See Clarke, 'Gothic Vibrations and Edgar Allan Poe', pp. 205–17.
[165] *The Black Tapes*, Episode 103.   [166] Sterne, *The Audible Past*, p. 2.

Gothic text during this time and beyond provides a darkly imagined underside to this rational and enlightened shaping of the aural sense. Inside the sound labyrinths of occluded Gothic spaces, the voice is a potential marker of identity, its timbre, pitch, accent and intonation, among other qualities, combining to form an auditory signature of subjectivity. Voice as a marker of coherent, even desirable, subjectivity is just one part of the audible spectrum of vococentric Gothic. Voices of ethical apparitions can be worked with to provide revelation, such as in the child's cries in Margaret Oliphant's 'The Open Door', or in Dickens's *A Christmas Carol*. Such threshold voices may always promise a secret but, like sirens calling, they can beckon towards death and destruction, too.

We find just such a harbinger of destruction in the apparition of Dickens's 'The Signal-Man' who stands not only literally at the threshold of a railway tunnel but figuratively seems to mark a temporal and fatalistic limit where present warnings cannot yet be translated into future action. This is the tragic element of the spectral voice – its status as a lament that cannot always effect change. Ghost speech and voice are thrown between and across characters in Dickens's late ghost story, and it is in the figure of 'voice throwing' that we find an apt metaphor for describing the echoing influence of Poe's vococentric soundworld of Gothic horror upon the writing of Robert Bloch, and via his *Psycho*, modern and contemporary horror too. The praxis of attentive listening, which is so important to uncovering the many mysteries of the Gothic romance, is eventually overwhelmed by vococentric horror, the moaner's hybrid cries in *Black Christmas* revealing nothing about his identity, only that he is pure drive and voice. The impossible voices of vococentric Gothic are hybrid, supernatural, monstrous and – as we discover in *The Black Tapes* – their effects are still echoing across contemporary media today.

Clearly, the numerous synaesthetic descriptions of Gothic voices that I have read across the main sections here suggest that there are elements of the auditory effects of voice that evade direct description as aural phenomena or, at least, which can only be written of metaphorically. Language reaches its limit and textuality strains to register the voice's own origins in sound. Even when an impossible voice can be heard rather than read – such as in *The Black Tapes* – its authenticity is placed in question: is this a counterfeit or the true unsound that we hear? Either way, any truly revealing representation of the unsound's suspected roots in pure voice seems always to be deferred. More clearly an authentic source of threat, the hybrid and monstrous voice in horror film produces a procession of abject sounds that suggest we are at a limit close to death; and this is one limit that cannot be traversed. The Gothic may be famed for its framed narratives that provide distance and a retrospective perspective on the terrors or horrors held within them, but vococentric Gothic disrupts these boundaries by the voice forcibly asserting its immediacy and presence. Such voices demand our attention be they spectral or monstrous. From the Gothic romance onwards, terror fiction often rewards attentive listeners with revelation and narrative resolution; modern and contemporary horror is rarely so generous.

References

Archambault, Angela M., 'The Function of Sound in the Gothic Novels of Ann Radcliffe, Matthew Lewis and Charles Maturin', *Études Épistémè* 29 (June 2016). http://journals.openedition.org/episteme/965.

Bae, Paul and Terry Miles, *The Black Tapes*, Episode 103 [Podcast] (2015–17). http://theblacktapespodcast.com/?offset=1441746399343.

Bailly, Lionel, *Lacan: A Beginner's Guide* (London: Oneworld, 2009).

Barrios-O'Neill, Danielle, 'Editor's Introduction to *Fearful Sounds: Cross-Platform Studies of Sonic Audio and Horror*', *Revenant Journal* special issue 3 (2018): 1–4.

Barthes, Roland, 'Textual analysis of a Tale by Edgar Poe', *Poe Studies (1971–1985)* 10:1 (1971): 1–12.

Beattie, James, *Essays on Poetry and Music, as They Affect the Mind*, 3rd ed. (London: E. and C. Dilly, 1779).

Beattie, James, 'Illustrations on Sublimity', in Rictor Norton (ed.), *Gothic Readings: The First Wave, 1764–1840* (London: Leicester University Press, 2000), pp. 283–5.

Berry, Richard, 'Podcasting: Considering the Evolution of the Medium and Its Association with the Word "Radio"', *The Radio Journal International Studies in Broadcast and Audio Media* 14:1 (2016): 7–22.

Bloch, Robert, 'The Man Who Collected Poe'. *Librarium* Cthulhuvius (2020). www.cthulhufiles.com/stories/bloch/bloch-the-man-who-collected-poe.html.

Bloch, Robert, *Psycho* (London: Robert Hale, 2013).

Bloch, Robert and Edgar Allan Poe, 'The Light-House', in Charles G. Waugh, Martin Harry Greenberg, and Jenny-Lynn Azarian (eds.), *Lighthouse Horrors: Tales of Adventure, Suspense, and the Supernatural* (Maine: Down East Books, 1993), pp. 153–68.

Botting, Fred, *Gothic*, 2nd ed. (London: Routledge, 2013).

Botting, Fred, 'Poe, Voice, and the Origin of Horror Fiction', in Jorge Sacido-Romero and Sylvia Mieszkowski (eds.), *Sound Effects: The Object Voice in Fiction* (Leiden: Brill Rodopi, 2015), pp. 73–100.

Brewster, David, *Letters on Natural Magic: Addressed to Sir Walter Scott* (London: John Murray, 1834).

Brewster, Scott, 'Extimacies: Strange Attachments in James Hogg, Robert Louis Stevenson, and Margaret Oliphant', *Gothic Studies* 24:1 (2022): 57–69.

Brockden Brown, Charles, *Wieland: Or, the Transformation: An American Tale*, ed. Emory Elliott (Oxford: Oxford University Press, 1998).

Cavalcanti, Alberto, Charles Crichton, Basil Dearden and Robert Hamer, dirs., *Dead of Night* (United Kingdom: Ealing Studios, 1945).

Chion, Michel, *The Voice in Cinema*, trans. Claudia Gorbman (New York: Columbia University Press, 1999).

Clark, Bob, dir., *Black Christmas* (Canada: Canadian Film Development Corporation, 1974).

Clarke, Frances, 'Gothic Vibrations and Edgar Allan Poe', *Horror Studies* 7:2 (2016): 205–17.

Coll, Fiona, '"Just a Singing-Machine": The Making of an Automaton in George du Maurier's *Trilby*', *University of Toronto Quarterly* 79:2 (Spring 2010): 742–63.

Connor, Steven, *Beyond Words: Sobs, Hums, Stutters and Other Vocalizations* (London: Reaktion Books, 2014).

Connor, Steven, *Dumbstruck: A Cultural History of Ventriloquism* (Oxford: Oxford University Press, 2000).

Connor, Steven, 'Whisper Music' (2008). *Steven Connor.* http://stevenconnor.com/whisper-music.html.

Constantineau, Sara, 'Black Christmas: The Slasher Film was Made in Canada', *CineAction* 82–83 (2011): 58+. *Gale General OneFile.* https://link.gale.com/apps/doc/A248407241/ITOF?u=mmucal5&sid=oclc&xid=381e7a35.

Crosby, Mark, 'The Voice of Flattery vs Sober Truth: William Godwin, Thomas Erskine and the 1792 Trial of Thomas Paine for Sedition', *The Review of English Studies* 62:253 (February 2011): 90–112.

Dacre, Charlotte, *Zofloya, Or the Moor: A Romance of the Fifteenth Century*, ed. Adriana Craciun (Peterborough: Broadview Press,1997).

Davies, Helen, *Gender and Ventriloquism in Victorian and Neo-Victorian Fiction: Passionate Puppets* (Houndmills: Palgrave Macmillan, 2012).

Dickens, Charles, *A Christmas Carol and Other Writings* (London: Penguin Books, 2003).

Dickens, Charles, *Complete Ghost Stories* (Hertfordshire: Wordsworth Editions, 2009).

Dolar, Mladen, 'Preface: Is There a Voice in the Text?', in Jorge Sacido-Romeo and Sylvia Mieszkowski (eds.), *Sound Effects: The Object Voice in Fiction* (Leiden: Brill Rodopi, 2015), pp. 11–20.

Dolar, Mladen, *A Voice and Nothing More* (Cambridge, MA: MIT Press, 2006).

Duncan, Ian, 'Scott's Ghost-Seeing', *Gothic Studies* 24:1 (2022): 44–56.

Fenimore, Ross J., 'Voices That Lie Within: The Heard and Unheard in *Psycho*', in Neil Lerner (ed.), *Music in the Horror Film: Listening to Fear* (New York: Routledge, 2010), pp. 80–97.

Fludernik, Monika, 'William Godwin's *Caleb Williams*: The Tarnishing of the Sublime', *ELH* 68:4 (2001): 857–96.

Foley, Matt, 'My Voice Shall Ring in Your Ears: The Acousmatic Voice and the Timbral Sublime in the Gothic Romance', *Horror Studies* 7:2 (2016): 173–88.

Foley, Matt, 'Tyranny as Demand', in Daniela Garofalo and David Sigler (eds.), *Lacan and Romanticism* (New York: State University of New York Press, 2019), pp. 141–56.

Frank, Adam, 'Valdemar's Tongue, Poe's Telegraphy', *ELH* 72:3 (2005): 635–62.

Friedkin, William, dir., *The Exorcist* (United States: Hoya Productions, 1973).

Galván, Fernando, 'Plagiarism in Poe: Revisiting the Poe-Dickens Relationship', *The Edgar Allan Poe Review* 10:2 (2009): 11–24.

Godwin, William, *Caleb Williams*, ed. David McCracken (Oxford: Oxford University Press, 1998).

Hancock, Dannielle and Leslie McMurtry, '"Cycles Upon Cycles, Stories Upon Stories": Contemporary Audio Media and Podcast Horror's New Frights', *Palgrave Communications* 3 (2017): 17075. https://doi.org/10.1057/palcomms .2017.75.

Hand, Richard J., *Listen in Terror: British Horror Radio from the Advent of Broadcasting to the Digital Age* (Manchester: Manchester University Press, 2014).

Hogg, James, *The Private Memoirs & Confessions of a Justified Sinner* (London: Vintage, 2010).

Joshi, S. T., *Unutterable Horror: A History of Supernatural Fictions*, 2 vols. (New York: Hippocampus Press, 2014).

Judson, Barbara, 'A Sound of Voices: The Ventriloquial Uncanny in *Wieland* and *Prometheus Unbound*', *Eighteenth-Century Studies* 44:1 (2010): 21–37.

Lagaay, Alice, 'Between Sound and Silence: Voice in the History of Psychoanalysis', *e-pisteme* 1:1 (2008): 53–63.

Lee, Vernon, *Hauntings and Other Fantastic Tales*, ed. Catherine Maxwell and Patricia Pulham (Peterborough: Broadview Press, 2006).

Leeder, Murray, *Horror Film: A Critical Introduction* (London: Bloomsbury, 2018).

Leighton, Angela, *Hearing Things: The Work of Sound in Literature* (Cambridge, MA: Harvard University Press, 2018).

Lewis, Matthew Gregory, *The Monk*, ed. Howard Anderson (Oxford: Oxford University Press, 2008).

Macdonald, D. L., '"A Dreadful Dreadful Dream": Transvaluation, Realization, and Literalization of *Clarissa* in *The Monk*', *Gothic Studies* 6:2 (2004): 157–71.

McAdams, Charity, *Poe and the Idea of Music: Failure, Transcendence, and Dark Romanticism* (Bethlehem: Lehigh University Press, 2017).

McMurtry, Leslie Grace, *Revolution in the Echo Chamber: Audio Drama's Past, Present and Future* (Bristol: Intellect Books, 2019).

Miles, Robert, *Ann Radcliffe: The Great Enchantress* (Manchester: Manchester University Press, 1995).

Morgan, Jack, *The Biology of Horror: Gothic Literature and Film* (Carbondale: Southern Illinois University Press, 2002).

Nash, Suzanne, 'The Appearances of "Monsieur Alexandre" in Firestone Library', *The Princeton University Library Chronicle* 74:3 (Spring 2013): 281–319.

Newman, Beth, 'Narratives of Seduction and the Seductions of Narrative: The Frame Structure of *Frankenstein*', *English Literary History* 53 (1986): 141–61.

O'Donnell, Patrick, '"A Speeches of Chaff": Ventriloquy and Expression in *Our Mutual Friend*', *Dickens Studies Annual* 19 (1990): 247–79.

OED, 'biloquist', n.: www.oed.com.ezproxy.mmu.ac.uk/view/Entry/19060?redirectedFrom=biloquist#eid. Last accessed: 13 June 2021.

Oliphant, Margaret, *The Open Door and Other Stories of the Seen and Unseen*, edited by Mike Ashley (London: The British Library, 2021).

Packham, Jimmy, *Gothic Utterance: Voice, Speech and Death in the American Gothic* (Cardiff: University of Wales Press, 2021).

Passey, Joan, 'The Aesthetics of the Auditory: Sound and Silence in the Novels of Ann Radcliffe', *Horror Studies*, 7:2 (2016): 189–204.

Peter Blatty, William. *The Exorcist* (London: Corgi, 2007).

Picker, John, *Victorian Soundscapes* (Oxford: Oxford University Press, 2003).

Pittard, Christopher, 'V for Ventriloquism: Powers of Vocal Mimicry in Henry Cockton's *The Life and Adventures of Valentine Vox, the Ventriloquist*', 19: *Interdisciplinary Studies in the Long Nineteenth Century* 24 (2017): https://19.bbk.ac.uk/article/id/1514/.

Poe, Edgar Allan, *Selected Poetry and Tales*, edited by James M. Hutchisson (Ontario: Broadview Press, 2012).

Pulham, Patricia, 'The Castrato and the Cry in Vernon Lee's Wicked Voices', *Victorian Literature and Culture* 30:2 (2002): 421–37.

Punter, David, 'Robert Bloch's *Psycho*: Some Pathological Contexts', in Brian Docherty (ed.), *American Horror Fiction: From Brockden Brown to Stephen King* (London: The MacMillan Press, 1990), pp. 92–106.

Radcliffe, Ann, *The Italian*, edited by Frederick Garber (Oxford: Oxford University Press, 1998).

Radcliffe, Ann, 'On The Supernatural in Poetry', in E. J. Clery and Roberts Miles (eds.), *Gothic Documents, A Sourcebook, 1700–1820* (Manchester: Manchester University Press, 2000), pp. 163–72.

Radcliffe, Ann, *A Sicilian Romance*, edited by Alison Milbank (Oxford: Oxford University Press, 2008).

Rajewsky, Irina O., 'Intermediality, Intertextuality, and Remediation: A Literary Perspective on Intermediality', *Intermédialités/Intermediality*, 6 (2005): 43–64.

Schlauraff, Kristie A., 'Victorian Gothic Soundscapes', *Literature Compass* 15:4 (2018): https://onlinelibrary.wiley.com/doi/full/10.1111/lic3.12445.

Scott, Sir Walter, *The Monastery* in *The Waverley Novels: Abbotsford Edition*, 12 vols (Philadelphia: J. B. Lippincott, 1877), vol. 5, pp. 5–264.

Scott, Sir Walter, *Letters on Demonology and Witchcraft* (London: Routledge, 1887).

Sterne, Jonathan, *The Audible Past* (Durham, NC: Duke University Press, 2003).

Stewart, David, 'Genuine Border Stories: James Hogg, Fiction and Mobility in the 1830s', *The Yearbook of English Studies* 48 (2018): 82–100.

Sweeney, Susan, 'Echoes of Ventriloquism in Poe's Tales', *Poe Studies: History, Theory, Interpretation*, 54:1 (2021): 127–55.

Toop, David, *Sinister Resonance: The Mediumship of the Listener* (London: Bloomsbury, 2010).

Townshend, Dale, 'Gothic Visions, Romantic Acoustics', *Romantic Circles*, December 2005. www.rc.umd.edu/praxis/gothic/townshend/townshend.

Thurston, Luke, 'Stories Not Like Any Others: Ghosts and the Ethics of Literature', in Scott Brewster and Luke Thurston (eds.), *The Routledge Handbook to the Ghost Story* (London: Routledge, 2017), pp. 467–75.

Van Elferen, Isabella, *Gothic Music: The Sounds of the Uncanny* (Cardiff: University of Wales Press, 2012).

Walpole, Horace, *The Castle of Otranto*, edited by Nick Groom (Oxford: Oxford University Press, 2014).

Weinstock, Jeffrey Andrew, 'Edgar Allan Poe and the Undeath of the Author', in Dennis R. Perry and Carl Hinckley Sederholm (eds.), *Adapting Poe: Re-Imaginings in Popular Culture* (New York: Palgrave Macmillan, 2012), pp.13–29.

Weinstock, Jeffery Andrew, 'Gothic and the New American Republic, 1770–1800', in Dale Townshend and Glennis Byron (eds.), *The Gothic World* (London: Routledge Books, 2014), pp. 27–37.

Weisse, Peter, 'The Object Voice in Romantic Irish Novels' in Jorge Sacido-Romero and Sylvia Mieszkowski (eds.), *Sound Effects: The Object Voice in Fiction* (Leiden: Brill Rodopi, 2015), pp. 47–71.

Wierzbicki, James, '*Psycho*-Analysis: Form and Function in Bernard Herrmann's Music for Hitchcock's Masterpiece', in Philip Hayward (ed.),

Terror Tracks: Music, Sound and Horror Cinema (London: Equinox, 2009), pp. 14–46.

Žižek, Slavoj, '"I Hear You with My Eyes"; or, The Invisible Master' in Renata Salecl and Slavoj Žižek (eds.), *Gaze and Voice as Love Objects* (New York: Duke University Press, 1996), pp. 90–126.

Žižek, Slavoj, *Enjoy Your Symptom!*, 2nd ed. (Routledge: London, 2001).

Acknowledgements

This Element would not have been possible without the dedication and support of the series editors Professors Dale Townshend and Angela Wright. I owe them both a debt of gratitude. Sincere thanks to the producers of *The Black Tapes* for allowing me to use their clip, as well as to Lucy Simpson, who assisted with editing the audio.

Cambridge Elements ≡

The Gothic

Dale Townshend
Manchester Metropolitan University
Dale Townshend is Professor of Gothic Literature in the Manchester Centre for Gothic Studies, Manchester Metropolitan University.

Angela Wright
University of Sheffield
Angela Wright is Professor of Romantic Literature in the School of English at the University of Sheffield and co-director of its Centre for the History of the Gothic.

Advisory Board

About the Series

Seeking to publish short, research-led yet accessible studies of the foundational 'elements' within Gothic Studies as well as showcasing new and emergent lines of scholarly enquiry, this innovative series brings to a range of specialist and non-specialist readers some of the most exciting developments in recent Gothic scholarship.

Cambridge Elements ≡

The Gothic

Elements in the Series

Gothic Voices: The Vococentric Soundworld of Gothic Writing
Matt Foley

A full series listing is available at: www.cambridge.org/GOTH

Printed in the USA
CPSIA information can be obtained
at www.ICGtesting.com
LVHW011303150324
774517LV00048B/2583